Music Crafts for Kids

The How-To Book of Music Discovery

Noel Fiarotta & Phyllis Fiarotta

Sterling Publishing Co., Inc. New York

Edited by Jeanette Green

Library of Congress Cataloging-in-Publication Data

Fiarotta, Noel.
    Music crafts for kids: the how-to book of music discovery / by
Noel Fiarotta & Phyllis Fiarotta.
      p.   cm.
    Includes index.
    ISBN 0-8069-0406-2
    1. Music—Instruction and study—Juvenile. 2. Musical
instruments—Construction—Juvenile. 3. Children's songs.
[1. Music. 2. Musical instruments—Construction.] I. Fiarotta,
Phyllis. II. Title.
MT740.F5 1993
372.87'044—dc20

93-24114
CIP
AC MN

2   4   6   8   10   9   7   5   3   1

Published in 1993 by Sterling Publishing Company, Inc.
387 Park Avenue South, New York, N.Y. 10016
© 1993 by Noel Fiarotta and Phyllis Fiarotta
Distributed in Canada by Sterling Publishing
% Canadian Manda Group, P.O. Box 920, Station U
Toronto, Ontario, Canada M8Z 5P9
Distributed in Great Britain and Europe by Cassell PLC
Villiers House, 41/47 Strand, London WC2N 5JE, England
Distributed in Australia by Capricorn Link Ltd.
P.O. Box 665, Lane Cove, NSW 2066
Manufactured in the United States of America

Sterling ISBN 0-8069-0406-2

Dedication

We dedicate this book to three masters of music who have enriched our lives with lovely melodies:

Our father, Anthony Fiarotta, who nurtured us with a daily dose of opera, ballet, band-shell concerts, and zarzuelas. And who believed, "without a song the day would never end." We deeply miss you.

Our grandfather, Natale Fiarotta, who taught us how to play our first notes, and composer of over a hundred mandolin compositions.

And our dear friend and teacher, George Hansler, professor of music, who has enriched our lives with a wealth of choral music. And who gathers those he loves and those who love him around the Christmas tree to sing and make merry.

Contents

The Magic of Music

When you were a baby, you made sounds with your voice to tell the world you were alive. You cried when hungry and you cooed when happy. As you grew older, you wanted to create more interesting sounds. You learned to clap your hands and shake your rattle. It wasn't long before you discovered that there was a wonderful world of music all around you.

It is hard for us to imagine a day pass without hearing a lively tune or singing a song. Music often makes you want to dance and sing. It also makes you feel better when things go wrong. Music is a powerful force that spins magic in our ears and hearts throughout our lives.

George Hansler, Ph.D.
Professor of Music, retired
Jersey City State College

Let the Music Begin

Welcome to *Music Crafts for Kids.* My name is **G Clef**. This book is filled with lots of fun facts, projects, and musical instruments you can make. Music began long ago when people first discovered the beat. This book takes you around the world to show you how that simple first beat developed into music, like the popular song "Mary Had a Little Lamb."

Musical instruments, dancing, composing music, singing, theater, and celebrations wait just pages away. Join me in a discovery of music. Your guide for each chapter will be one of the eight musical notes that live on a scale and some of their friends. I am happy to turn over the first chapter of your musical adventure to my good friend, **Do**.

NATURE'S
MUSIC

Sounds of the Earth

 Hi! I'm **Do**. Join me in discovering the music of the Earth. From the lowest valleys to the highest mountain tops, in the oceans below and in the sky above, natural sounds abound.

Rivers and streams make different sounds. When they plunge as waterfalls, the sound is thunderous. When they flow over rocks, they babble and gurgle.

Rain rat-tat-tats on umbrellas, splish-splashes in puddles, and plop-plops on the roof.

The oceans have waves caused by rising and dropping tides and by storms. Waves can gently splash on sandy beaches or roughly crash onto rocky coastlines.

Gentle breezes can barely be heard. The blustery winds of tornadoes and hurricanes roar and whistle.

The music of wind flutters when it blows against flags or the sails of ships. Breezes blowing through tree leaves make rustling sounds.

Last, but not least, are the songs of the birds and animals of the Earth. The birds chirp, the lions roar, the wolves howl, the cows moo, and the rattle snake plays music with its tail.

Fluttering Streamer

The wind is a force that makes flags flutter. You can be a mighty force like the wind and create your own fluttering sounds.

Things You Need
wooden spoon or stick
roll of crêpe paper streamer

Tie a crêpe paper streamer to a wooden spoon or stick. The streamer should be about twice your height.

Here are some ways to make the streamer flutter:

Make figure 8's.
Make wide circles above your head.
Snap it sharply back and forth.
Wave it gently and snap it sharply.
Twirl two streamers at one time.
Tie two or more crêpe paper lengths to one stick.
Experiment with streamers of different lengths.

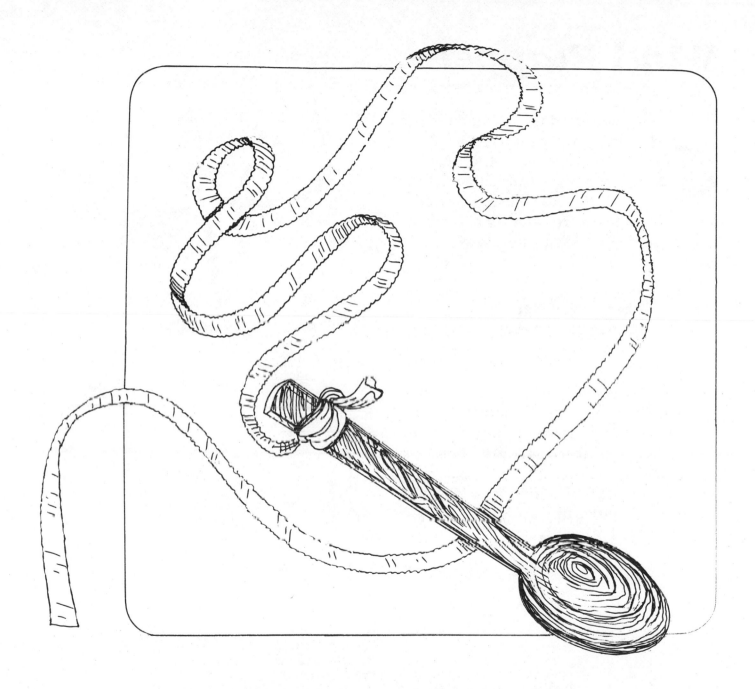

Wind Flapper

The windmills of Holland are like big pinwheels. They catch breezes which can be used as wind power. Pinwheels also create energy when they spin. Here is a way to hear the mighty force of a spinning pinwheel.

Things You Need
pinwheel • paper

1. Cut a small piece of paper.
2. Hold the pinwheel in the wind.
3. Hold the paper near the pinwheel. As the pinwheel spins, allow its points to scrape the paper.
4. Experiment with different weights of paper, plastic, and foil. Blow on the pinwheel both softly and forcefully.

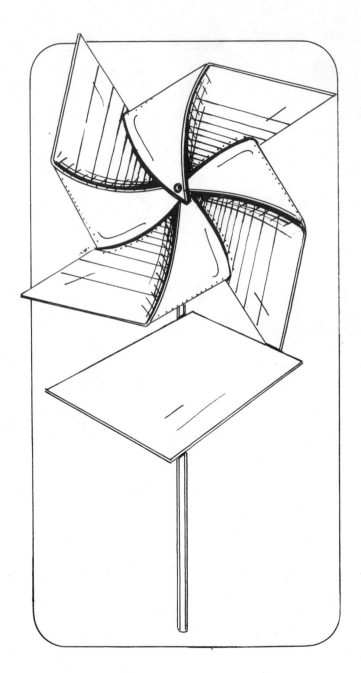

Cave Winds

A cave is a hole in the ground or in a mountain. Winds blowing into a cave create eerie, hollow sounds. The sounds change from cave to cave, depending on how deep each is. Think of a bottle as a mini-cave and your breath as the gusty wind that gives it a voice.

Things You Need
bottles

Here are many things you can do to create cave winds:

Blow over the opening.
Place your bottom lip against the opening and puff into the bottle.
Blow into the bottle from different angles.
Blow into bottles of different shapes and sizes.
Blow into bottles filled with different levels of water.

Wind Chimes

When wind knocks things together, it produces sounds. This wind chime has a tool chest of dangling nails and screws. Hang it in a window, in a tree, or on a fire escape to hear the clinks, clanks, and tings.

Things You Need
plastic coffee can lid
paper punch • cord
assorted large screws and nails

1. With a paper punch, make four holes in a plastic lid equally spaced from each other (a). You can also make holes in the lid with a large nail using a twisting motion. Ask an adult to help you.
2. Cut two long cords for hanging.
3. Feed the cord through the holes. Study b.
4. Make the ends of the cords even and knot each cord (c).
5. Punch more holes into the lid (d). Scatter the holes all around.
6. Tie cords to the heads of large screws and nails (e).
7. Push the cord ends through the holes on the lid and knot them (f). The knots should be big enough so that they don't slip through the holes.

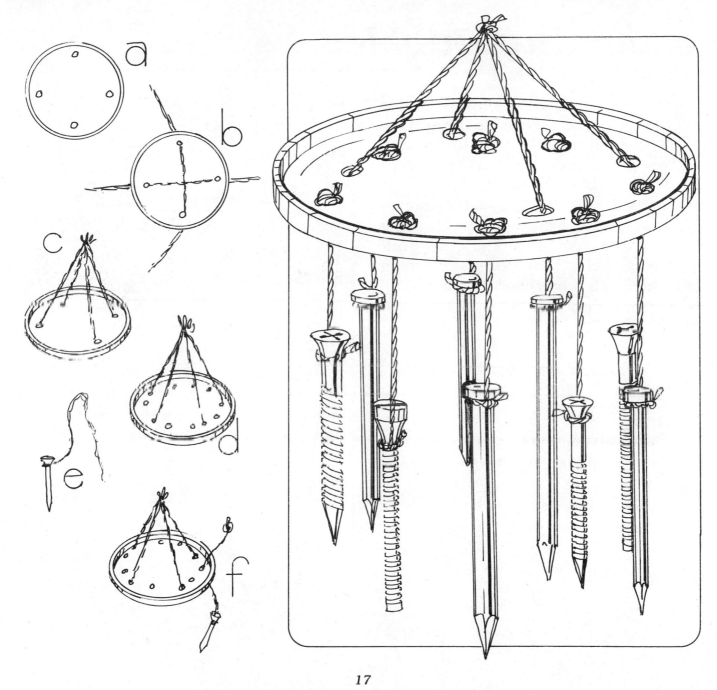

a

b

c

d

e

f

17

Humming Bubbles

When air escapes under water, it rises to the surface as bubbles. Bubbles are also created when water splish-splashes about.

The canary whistle is an old-fashioned toy that uses splashing water. It looks like a bubble pipe. You fill the whistle full of water and blow into it to make chirping sounds. Create a fish chorus of humming bubbles with just a straw and a glass of water.

Things You Need
drinking glass
drinking straw • water

1. Place a straw in a glass of water.
2. Blow into the straw while humming a song.

Raindrop Catchers

 Every time it rains, nature entertains us with sounds. Here is how you can capture the music of raindrops.

Things You Need

assortment of pots, pans, trays, and dishes

Set rain catchers on a window ledge, a front stoop, a back porch, or a fire escape. They should be placed where you can hear the sounds raindrops make without getting wet.

Compare the sounds raindrops make when they hit catchers made of different materials, such as metal, paper, glass, china, plastic, or foam

Observe the different sounds raindrops make when the catchers are empty and after they have collected some puddles.

Write down words that best describe the sounds the raindrops make. Do they *ping, ting,* or *plop*?

Echoes

 If you live in a valley or near a mountain and yell as loud as you can. Sometimes you can hear your voice repeat over and over. This is called an echo. You can hear the wonder of echoes without leaving home. It's easy to do. It's a small matter of angles and a ticking clock . . . a ticking clock . . . a ticking clock.

Things You Need
2 paper towel tubes • heavy paper
ticking watch *or* small clock

1. Lay down one tube at the edge of a table (a).

2. Cut out a piece of heavy paper about the size of this book. Fold it in half.

3. Stand the paper at the opposite end of the tube on the table (b). Place the end of the tube as close to the paper as possible without touching it.

4. Lay down the second tube on the table. Place it as close to the other side of the standing paper as possible, without touching it (c).

5. Place a ticking watch at the end of the second tube.

6. Put your ear at the end of the first tube at the table's edge (a). Can you hear the ticking sound? If not, change the angles of the tube until you hear the ticking as clearly as possible. The angles of the two tubes need to be equal to each other, so that you can hear the echo.

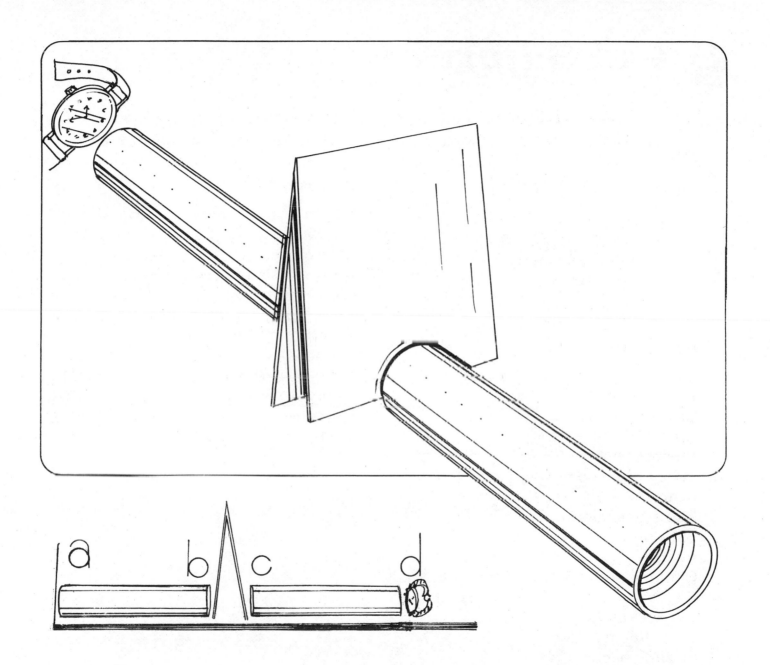

Sound Safari

 I've told you about many musical sounds of the Earth. Now it's time for you to go on a sound safari to hunt for others. Hike into the woods for natural sounds, walk down a city street for sounds people make, and explore your home for family sounds. And don't forget your father's snoring.

Walking Tours

1. Walk into the woods. Listen for:
   Chirping birds
   Croaking bullfrogs
   Rustling tree leaves
   Stepping on dry leaves
2. Take a walk down a city street. You'll hear:
   Blaring car horns
   Barking dogs
   Roaring jet planes
   Clinking and clanking of construction
3. Explore your own house. Here are some sounds:
   Tumbling door locks
   Sizzling bacon

Humming electrical appliances
Bleeps and beeps of video games

More Sound Ideas

1. Open a faucet to create a wide range of water sounds from drips to full-force streams. Don't forget the spraying sounds you hear in the shower.
2. Hold paper, fabric, or plastic in front of a spinning fan to create different fluttering sounds.
3. Drop all sorts of things onto surfaces like a wooden table or a ceramic tile floor to create different striking sounds. Just be sure what you drop isn't breakable!

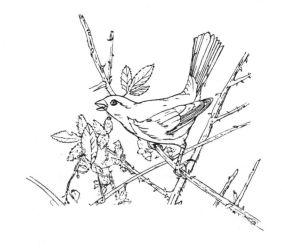

THE BIRTH OF THE BEAT

The First Noisemakers

 Welcome. I'm **Re**, your time-travel guide. Come with me to see how early humans discovered the beat in the natural music of the Earth. They found that beat in barking dogs, in falling raindrops, and in their heartbeats.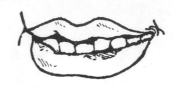

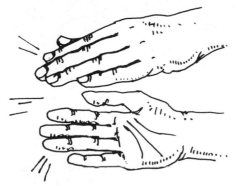

Early people began making noises with their bodies. They sang in grunts and groans. They made other simple body sounds by snapping their fingers and stomping their feet.

Eventually early people found out that clapping their hands together was an easy way to make different beats.

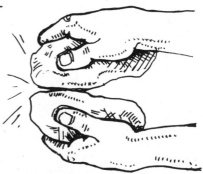

Finally they discovered that holding things in their hands and striking them created a variety of sounds. Stones may have been the first musical instruments.

Other musical instruments were probably found close to home. Early people experimented with different objects to create sounds. Hitting two long sticks together made a better sound than hitting two twigs. Hitting pine cones made a softer sound than hitting bones.

Early people who lived by the sea made different sounds than people who lived in the woods. That's because they had different materials. They could blow into a large shell to create an early horn. They could click shells together as early castanets.

Log Drum

Early people found out that beating a hollow log made more noise than beating a solid log. Hollow logs were used to send messages between villages. Log drums are still used in many parts of the world to make music.

Things You Need

3 or more large fruit juice cans
strong tape
brown paper or large brown
grocery bags
scissors • crayons or markers
green paper • 2 sticks

1. Remove both ends from three or more cans (a). Ask an adult to help.
2. Tape the cans together to form a log (b).
3. Cut out enough brown paper to wrap around the log. You may need two or more sheets to cover the log. Brown grocery bags work well.
4. Roll the paper around the log and tape it in place (c).
5. Draw a wood grain design on the brown paper with crayons or markers (d).
6. Cut out several leaves from green paper.
7. Tape the leaves underneath your log (e).
8. Strike the log with the sticks to create sounds.

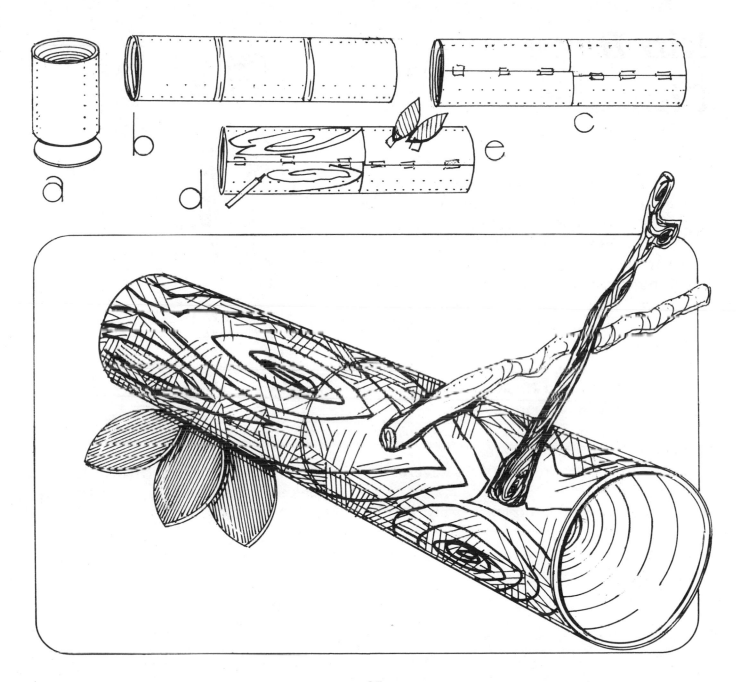

a

b

c

d

e

27

Rib Bone Clappers

 Clappers are two objects that have the same shape and can be hit together to make sounds. Early people probably used animal bones as musical instruments. Later, in old traveling shows, many American entertainers danced, and clicked rib bones in their hands. These entertainers were called minstrels.

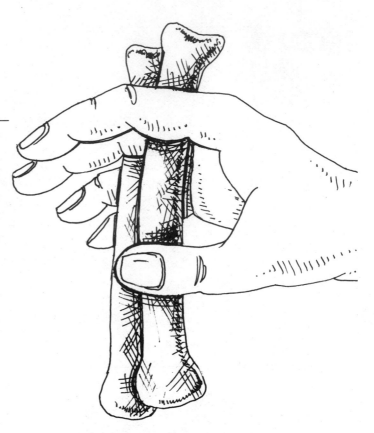

Things You Need
2 spare rib bones

1. Scrub clean two rib bones.
2. Allow the bones to dry out for several days.
3. To play, hold the bones loosely between your fingers in one hand. Shake or rattle them together. Use the thumb at times.

Sand Scraping

 Early people found out that when they walked on sand, their feet made scraping sounds. You've probably noticed this at the beach. Musicians today make similar sounds when they accompany music with sandpaper attached to wooden blocks. Here is a simple way to create your own scraping beats.

Things You Need
sandpaper • newspaper
old wooden or metal spoon or fork

1. Choose fine, medium, or coarse sandpaper. Each will make a different sound.
2. Lay a sheet of sandpaper on a sheet of newspaper. The newspaper will catch any grains of sand that come loose from the sandpaper.
3. Scrape the sandpaper with a fork or spoon. Create a beat or accompany a song.

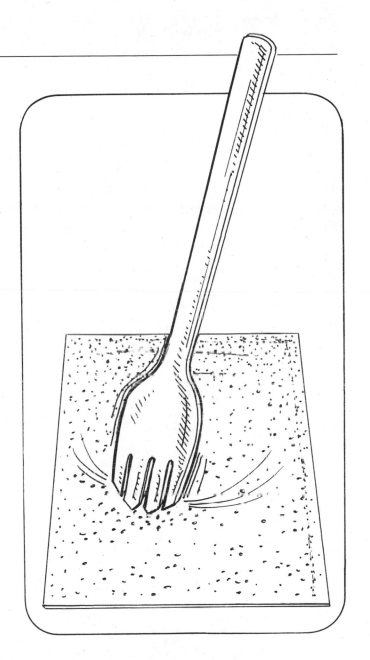

Buzz Disk

The bull-roarer is a disk attached to a string that makes a roaring sound when spun. Bull-roarers have been used in Australia, New Guinea, Brazil, North and South America, and other places. People used the noise of the bull-roarer to drive fish up narrow streams and to chase animals into nets. Early humans probably used sea shells and vines to create bull-roarers to scare away wild wolves prowling around their cooking fires. This buzz disk is a cousin of the bull-roarer.

Things You Need

heavy cardboard • drinking glass
scissors • nail • glue • cord

1. On cardboard, trace around the open end of a drinking glass. Draw two circles and cut them out.

2. Divide one circle into four equal parts (a).

3. Divide one part into two equal sections. See the heavy dashed lines in (a). Cut out to form wedges.

4. Twist two holes into the uncut circle using a large nail (b). Ask an adult to help you. It is important to center the two holes on the circle.

5. Glue the wedges to the circle with the points between the two punched holes (c).

6. Feed the ends of a long cord through the holes and knot them. Even up the cord so that you have an equal amount on both sides.

7. To make the disk buzz, place the cord ends over your middle fingers. Spin the disk until the cord is tightly wound. Then jerk your hands apart. The disk will unwind rapidly, making a humming sound.

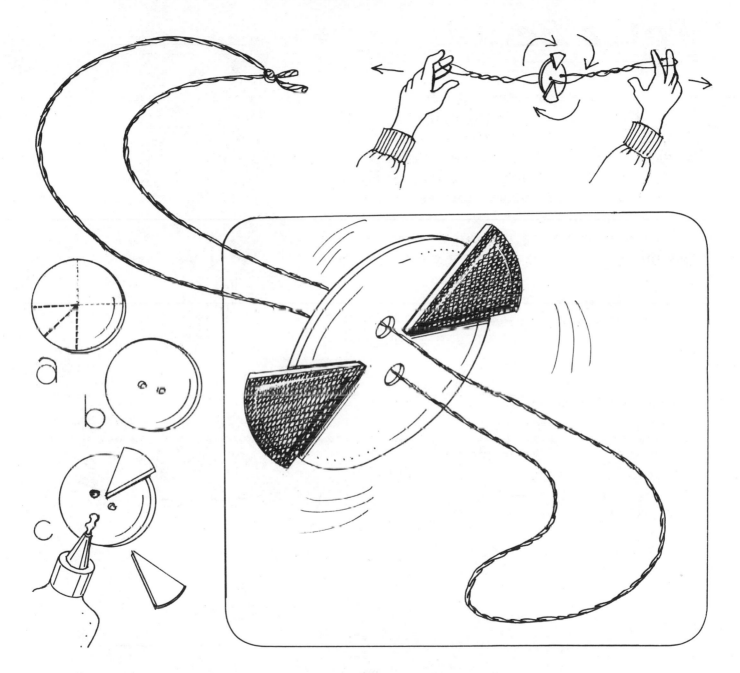

Water Beats

Early humans caught fish in shallow pools by slapping the water to drive the fish into waiting hands. When the fish didn't cooperate, perhaps the people created interesting rhythms and beats. You may not want to coax a fish into a frying pan, but you will enjoy making music in a bowl of water.

Things You Need
bowl • water • towel

1. Fill a bowl with water. If you are not outdoors, place the bowl on a towel to protect the floor or furniture.
2. Create water rhythms by:

   Moving your fingers rapidly
   Slapping the water with the palm of your hand
   Flicking your fingers

Mouth Drum

We think early humans spoke in grunts and groans. Perhaps they discovered that the mouth could make other sounds, the same way a drum does. By hitting their cheeks while opening and closing their lips, they could make all sorts of popping sounds. You can, too.

Things You Need

mouth • hands

Open you mouth. Lightly hit your cheeks with your open hands. It works best when your hands are straight and your fingers are together.

Create different sounds by:

Opening and closing your mouth
Tightening your lips in a pucker
Hitting your cheeks lightly and force-
fully

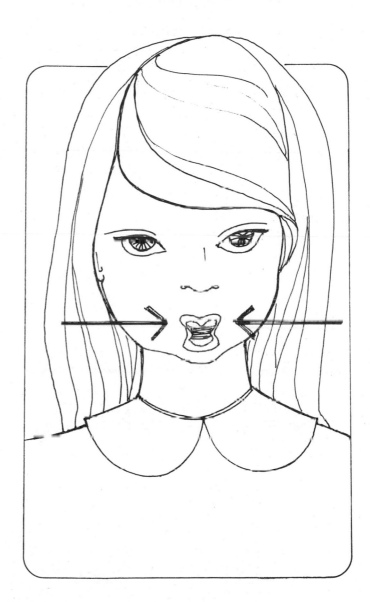

Gourd Rattle

Gourds are very colorful squashes. Early people discovered that gourds, left to dry out in the sun, rattled when they were shaken. The rattling sounds came from the dried seeds inside the gourds. Gourd rattles probably added musical beats to early songs.

Things You Need
balloon • masking tape • paste
newspaper • waxed paper • knife
dried rice or beans • paints
paintbrush

1. Blow up a balloon and knot the neck (a).
2. To give the balloon a gourd shape, wrap tape around the end with the neck (b).
3. Rip newspaper into small strips.
4. Place the strips on a sheet of waxed paper. Spread glue on the top sides (c).
5. Cover the entire balloon with three layers of newspaper strips (d). Dry.
6. Cut away the neck of the wrapped balloon plus a little of the paper, creating a small opening (e). Remove the balloon. Ask an adult to help you.
7. Add dried rice or beans through the neck of your gourd (f).
8. Cover the neck hole with glued newspaper strips (g).
9. Paint the gourd rattle in yellows, browns, and greens. Add stripes and dots.
10. Hold the narrow end and shake.

You could also try drying a gourd. Hang it by a string for several months to dry. Then you can paint or decorate it.

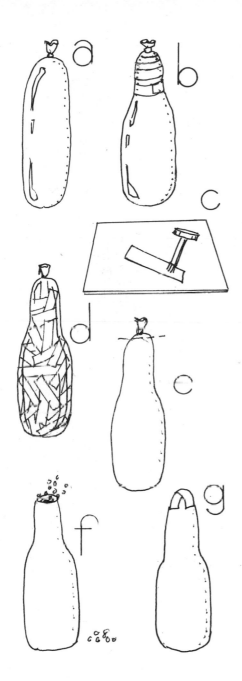

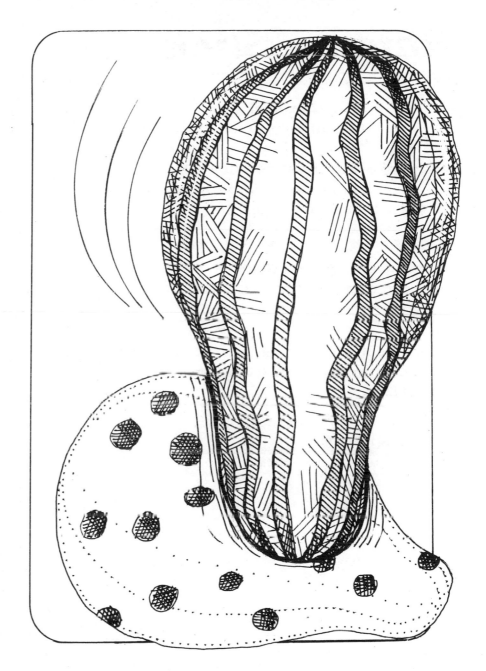

Rhythm Sticks

 Rhythm sticks are real instruments used by musicians. They are one of the simplest musical instruments, and people have used them for thousands of years.

Things You Need

2 identical or similar objects

Experiment with sounds by striking two identical things or two objects of the same size.

Wooden spoon and fork (A)
Two sticks (B)
Metal spoon and fork (C)

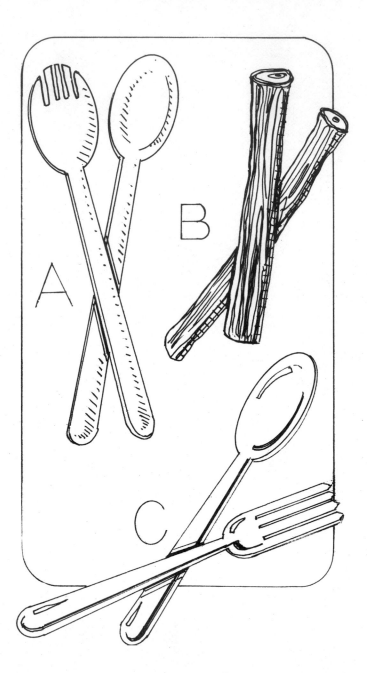

PLUCK, BOW, BANG & BLOW

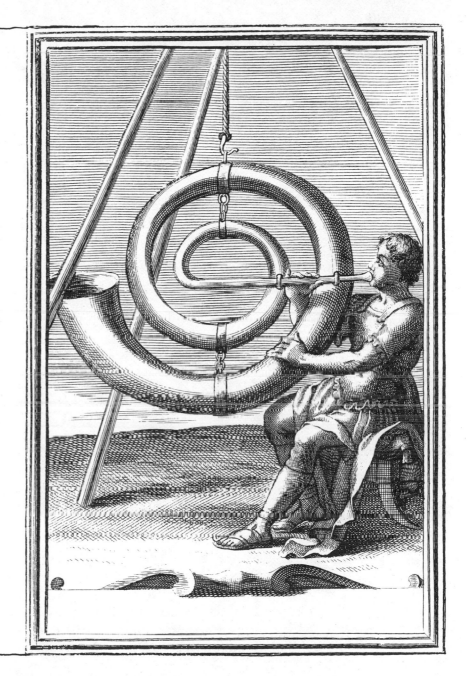

Early Musical Instruments

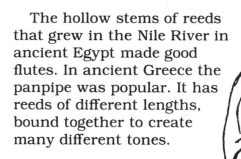

 Howdy! I'm **Mi**. No, not me, *Mi*. Musical instruments have changed a lot since early humans banged two sticks together or beat a hollow log. Let's explore the history of early musical instruments.

The hollow stems of reeds that grew in the Nile River in ancient Egypt made good flutes. In ancient Greece the panpipe was popular. It has reeds of different lengths, bound together to create many different tones.

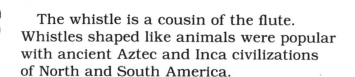

The whistle is a cousin of the flute. Whistles shaped like animals were popular with ancient Aztec and Inca civilizations of North and South America.

In New Guinea today, native people play log drums that look the same as they did thousands of years ago.

Harps were played in Egypt as early as 3000 B.C.E. The Romans and Greeks played harps when singing songs of love and lore.

Although most people think the bagpipe comes from Scotland, it was actually invented by early Romans. Soldiers carried them into battle.

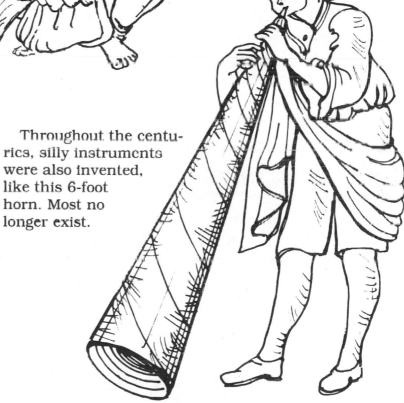

Throughout the centuries, silly instruments were also invented, like this 6-foot horn. Most no longer exist.

Skin Drum

 The first drums were hollow logs, which were struck to make sounds. Eventually, animal skins were stretched over the openings of the logs. Then, the skins, instead of logs, were hit to make sounds.

People, all over the world, play their own special drums. Some Africans use talking drums. Many people in Latin American bang on bongos. This Native American tom-tom is decorated with brave warriors hunting a buffalo.

Things You Need

large fruit juice can • colored paper
scissors • crayons or markers
tape or paste
waxed paper or soft vinyl
2 strong rubber bands • 2 corks
2 pencils

1. Remove the top and bottom of a juice can (a). Ask an adult to help you.
2. Cut colored paper that's as tall as the can and long enough to wrap around it.
3. With crayons or markers, draw Native Americans hunting buffalo on the paper (b).
4. Tape or paste the paper to the can (c).
5. Cut two circles from waxed paper or vinyl (d). The circles should be larger than the opening of the can.
6. Place a paper or vinyl circle over an opening (e).
7. Fold over the excess paper or vinyl. Attach the circle to the can with a rubber band (f). If the paper is not tight, wrap the elastic band around the can a second time.
8. Cover the other end of the can as you did the first.
9. To make drumsticks, twist the sharpened points of two pencils into corks.

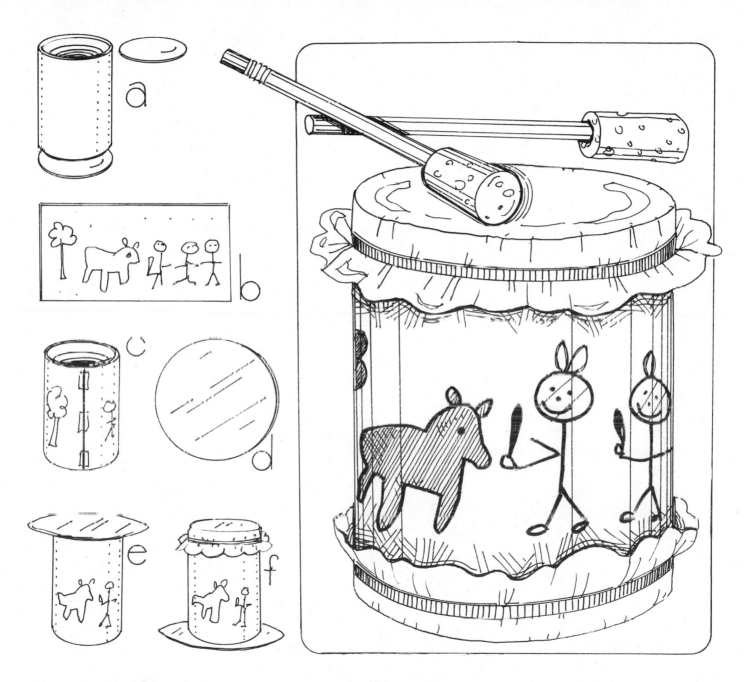

Mouth Bow

The mouth bow is a combination of the mouth drum and a one-string instrument. People have played mouth bows more than 17,000 years. And some people still play them today.

Things You Need
3 feet of narrow wood lattice or a
lightweight yardstick
small saw • drill
fishing line (50-pound test)

For this project, ask an adult to help you.

1. Cut three notches into each end of the lattice or yardstick with a saw. Study a.
2. Drill a hole into each end (see a).
3. Tie one end of a long fishing line to one end of the lattice. Go into the notches and through the hole. Be sure you make a tight knot. See b.
4. Pull the line taut to make the lattice curve. Tie and line tightly to the other end of the lattice.

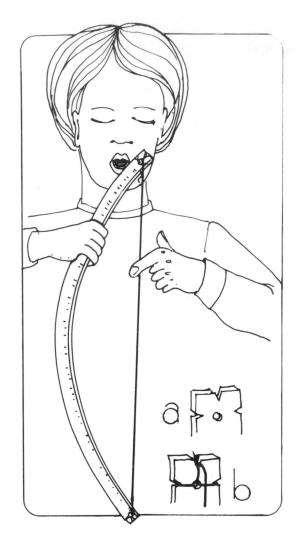

5. To play, hold the end of the bow against your partially opened and tensed mouth. Pluck the string with a fingernail or guitar pick. Change the shape of your mouth to create soft melodies.

Clay Whistle

Whistles have been used ever since people made clay pottery. The Inca and Aztec civilizations of North and South America made clay whistles shaped like animals and birds. Here is a whistle that will make you whistle up a storm.

Things You Need
measuring cup • salt • water
flour • saucepan • mixing spoon
cookie sheet • small whistle
lentils or beads

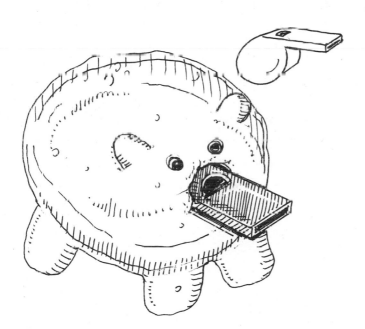

1. Mix 1 cup of water, ½ cup of flour, and 1 cup of salt in a saucepan.
2. Heat the mixture on the stove over low heat. Stir continually until it is thick and rubbery. Ask an adult to help you.
3. Empty the clay on a floured cookie sheet.
4. Roll half the clay into a ball around a whistle. The mouthpiece should extend out of the clay. The opening should not be covered with clay.
5. Pinch and pull the clay to create legs, wings, a tail, and ears.
6. Use lentils or small beads for eyes.
7. Allow the clay to dry before using.

Native American Rattle

Native Americans still use rattles during ceremonial chants and dances. They often attached beads to the rattles to add jingling sounds. Feathers and rawhide streamers add decorative touches. Shake this rattle for an authentic sound.

Things You Need
plastic dishwashing
detergent bottle
stick or wide wooden dowel •
scissors • rice or dried beans
fabric or paper • white liquid glue
cardboard • ribbon • feathers
beads

1. Remove the label from a washed liquid detergent bottle.
2. Find a stick longer than the bottle. (It should fit snugly in the neck.)
3. Ask an adult to cut a hole into the bottom of the bottle (a). It should be in the center and a little smaller than the width of the stick.
4. Tilt the bottle and add dried beans (b).
5. Push the stick through the neck and out the hole (c).
6. Glue a strip of fabric or paper around the neck and part of the stick (d).
7. Squeeze glue around the other end of the stick, where it touches the bottle (e). Dry.
8. Decorate with ribbons tied around the stick. Tuck feathers into the knot (f). Add a string of beads, if you like.

45

Bagpipe

Bagpipes have been played for more than 1,000 years. Some early bagpipes were heart-shaped sacks. Others were made from the entire skins of pigs. Bagpipes make sounds when air is forced out of the bag and into the pipes. Today bagpipes are played in Asia, North Africa, and Europe. We know Scottish bagpipes best.

Things You Need
plastic bag • party horn • cord

1. Blow up a plastic bag. The bigger the bag the longer you can play your bagpipe.
2. Slip the mouthpiece of a party horn into the open end of the bag. Be careful not to let too much air escape.
3. Tie the bag tightly to the horn with cord. It will be easier if someone helps you.
4. To play the bagpipe, press the bag to force air into the horn. Depending on the horn, you may be able to blow up the bag again through the horn without untying it.

Straw Oboe

The oboe is a long, black musical instrument. It has a mouthpiece made of two thin pieces of bamboo that are called reeds. The instrument creates sounds when air passes between the reeds and they move back and forth. This straw oboe is a simple double-reed instrument.

Things You Need
plastic drinking straw • scissors

1. Pinch one end of the drinking straw flat.
2. Cut the end of the straw into a point to form the double reeds.
3. To play your straw oboe, put the reed end of the straw into your mouth, just behind your lips, and blow *very* hard. It may take several tries to make the oboe work.
4. Create different sounds by cutting straws into different lengths. Also, cut the points longer or shorter.

Gourd Scraper

 Do you know what *idiophones* are? They are instruments that are struck, rung, shook, or scraped. The musical instruments that early humans used were idiophones, like sticks, stones, and bones. In last chapter my brother Re showed you how people used dried gourds as rattles. Dried gourds were also used as scraped instruments. Add a beat to a favorite song with this Latin American sound.

Things You Need

long balloon • newspaper • scissors
paste • waxed paper • heavy cord
white liquid glue • paper cup
paintbrush • paints

1. Blow up a balloon. Knot the neck.
2. Tear newspaper into small strips.
3. Place the strips on waxed paper and brush paste on one side of them (a).
4. Cover the entire balloon with three layers of these strips (b).
5. Tie a long cord to the neck of the balloon (c).
6. Coil the cord evenly spaced around the balloon (d). Tuck the end into the wrapped cord. Cut away the remaining cord (e).
7. Pour white liquid glue into a paper cup.
8. Paint the newspaper and cord with a thick coating of glue (f).
9. Cut away the neck of the balloon. Paint the gourd a bright color (g). Add colorful designs.
10. Scrape a stick or an old wooden spoon up and down the gourd.

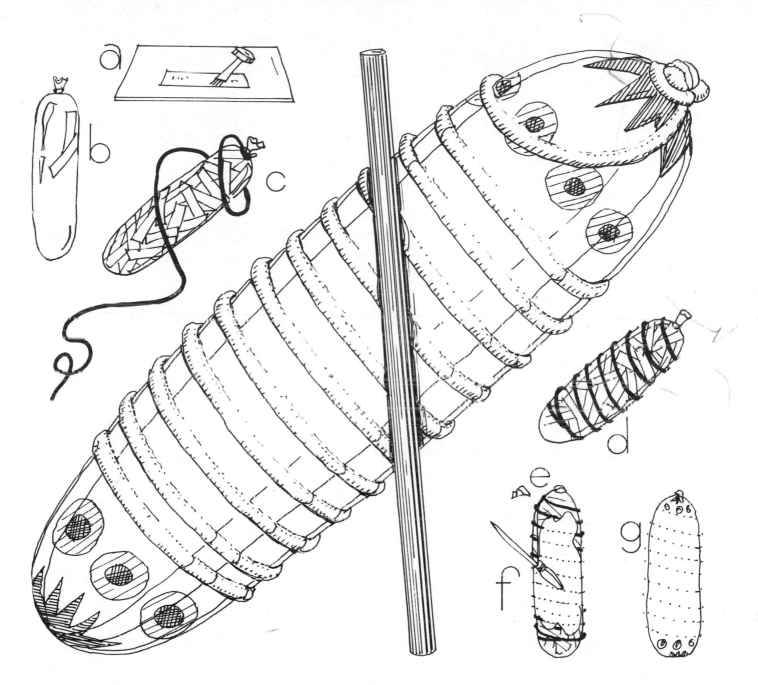

49

African Lyre

The lyre was popular in ancient Greece. One kind had strings and a sound box made from a turtle shell. In Greek mythology, Apollo and Orpheus played the lyre. In Africa, the lyre is still used to accompany songs in festivals and ceremonies. This lyre does not make sounds, but it will be a nice decoration for your room.

Things You Need
round balloon • newspaper
scissors • paste • waxed paper
3 sticks the same size • scissors
paint • paintbrush • colored yarn
feathers • beads

1. Blow up a round balloon. Knot the neck (a).
2. Tear newspaper into small strips.
3. Place the strips on waxed paper and brush paste on one side (b).
4. Cover the entire balloon with three layers of pasted strips. Also cover the neck with strips (c).
5. To form the lyre's sound box, flatten half of the covered balloon by pressing it on waxed paper on a table (d). Study the drawing to see where the neck should be. If the *sound box* does not hold its shape, twist a sharpened pencil through the newspaper to break the balloon inside. (See arrow in d.) Handle it gently after the balloon is broken. Dry.
6. Attach the ends of two sticks to the flat side of the sound box with glued paper strips (e). The sticks should be opposite the neck and flair out a little.
7. Cut out two round holes below the sticks with scissors (f).
8. Tie the third stick to the first two with yarn (g).
9. Tie two long colored yarns to the neck (h).
10. Tie the ends of the yarn to the cross stick. Cut away the extra yarn.
11. Paint the sound box and attach feathers and beads.

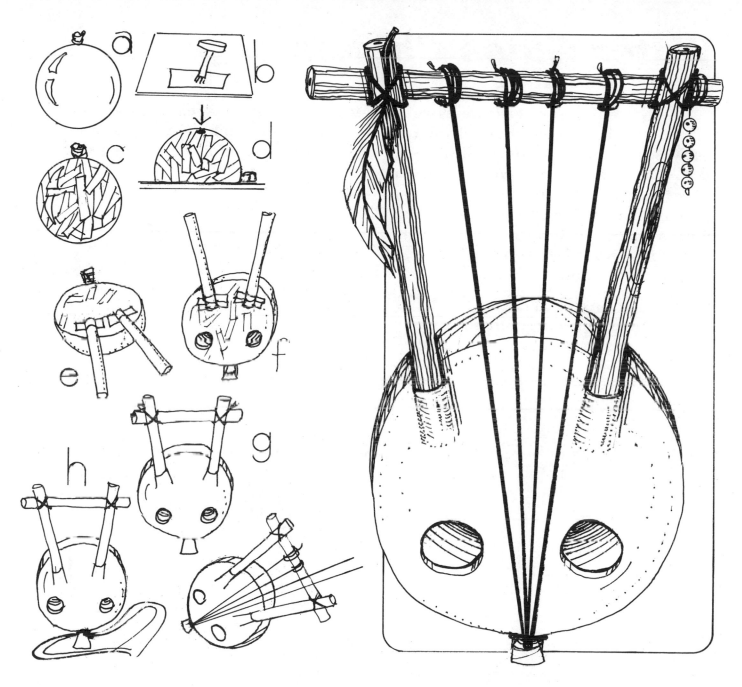

51

Water Glass Chimes

Chimes and bells were two of the earliest musical instruments. Made in different sizes, they produce low to high sounds when struck. Bells are still used in church towers, and chimes are used in clocks. You can easily turn drinking glasses into musical chimes. Here's how.

1. Fill the drinking glasses with different levels of water—from nearly empty to almost full.

2. Strike the glasses with a wooden spoon or stick. If you have eight glasses, try to play a simple song.

Things You Need
6 to 8 drinking glasses the same size
water • wooden spoon or stick

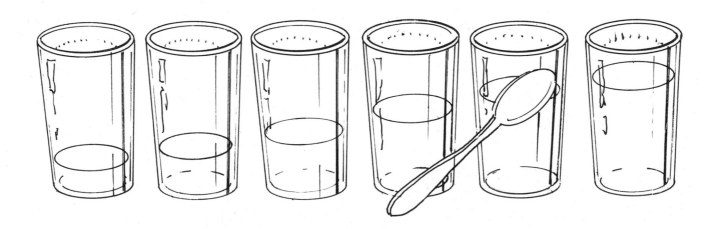

THE EIGHT LITTLE NOTES

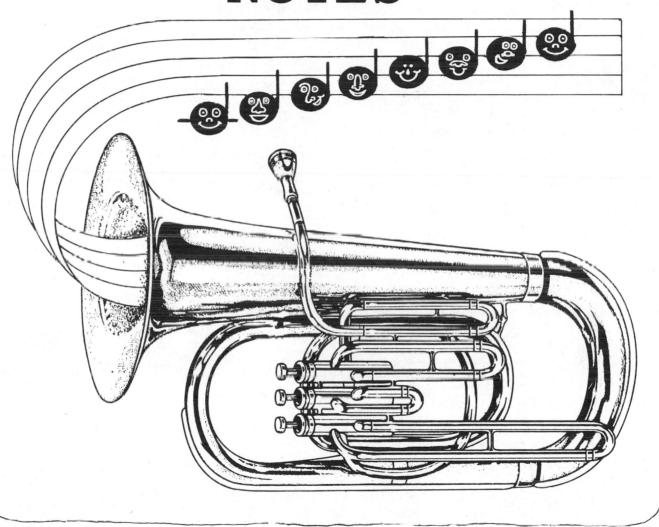

Notable Facts

Hi! I'm **Fa**, the fourth note. My brother and sister notes were not always shaped like eggs. We've had many different shapes, and they have sat on many different parallel lines called staffs. Come with me on a brief tour of my family history.

In the very beginning, notes were not written on staffs. They were drawn under the words of songs. Early church music was written on staffs with four lines. The notes are square because they were drawn with pens that had square points. Eventually, a fifth line was added to the staff. Some notes were drawn as diamond shapes.

A handy way to teach music is using the hand. Music teachers once pointed to the joints of the left hand, where the names of notes were written. The pupils then sang the right notes.

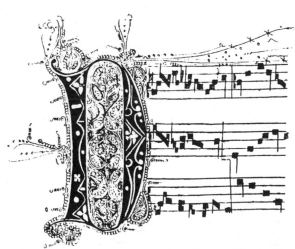

Beautiful letters and drawings
were painted on early sheet music.

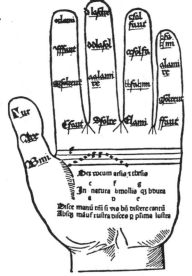

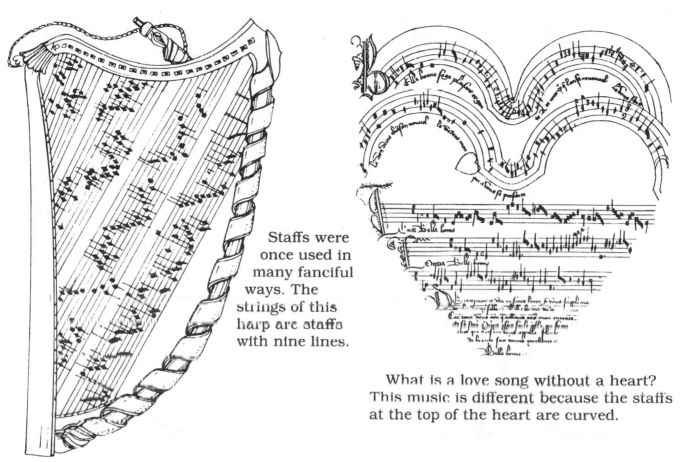

Staffs were once used in many fanciful ways. The strings of this harp are staffs with nine lines.

What is a love song without a heart? This music is different because the staffs at the top of the heart are curved.

The look of written music has changed through the years. These three staffs show music from the earliest days to the present.

We're the Note Family

I'd like you to meet my brothers and sisters: **DO** (*doh*), **RE** (*ray*), **MI** (*mee*), **SO** (*so*), **LA** (*lah*), **TI** (*tee*), and DO's twin brother, **DO** (*doh*). And don't forget, I'm **FA** (*fah*). This is how we look when we are **quarter notes**. We are solid black with stems.

When we are quarter notes, each one of us has one **beat** of music. If you clap your hands one time, that is a beat. If you clap two or more times, you have made a series of beats called a **rhythm**. Our smiles tell you we love music.

I will demonstrate how we look when we wear our other faces (p. 57).

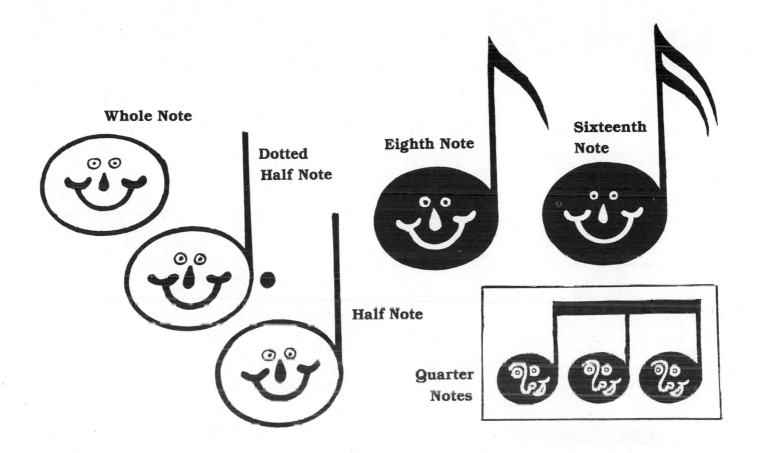

Whole Note

Dotted Half Note

Eighth Note

Sixteenth Note

Half Note

Quarter Notes

Whole Note is an open note. It has 4 beats.
Dotted Half Note is an open note with a stem and a dot. It has 3 beats.
Half Note is an open note with a stem. It has 2 beats.
Quarter Note is a black note with a stem. It has 1 beat.

Eighth Note is a black note with a stem and a flag. It has ½ beat.
Sixteenth Note is a black note with a stem and two flags. It has ¼ beat.

Sometimes eighth notes and sixteenth notes are joined together by their flags.

The Staff

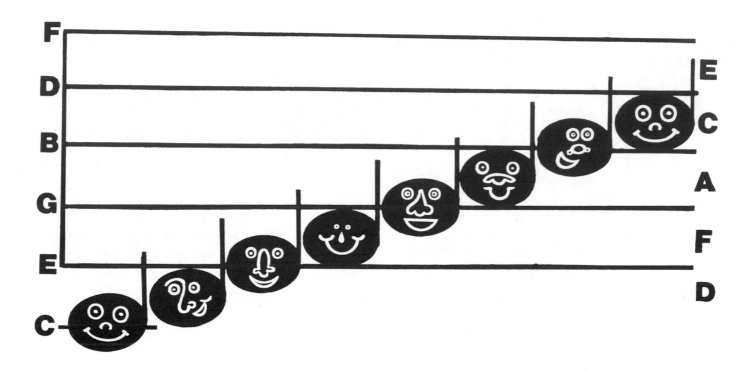

Now that you've been introduced to the Note family's many personalities, I'd like to show you where Do, Re, Fa, So, La, Ti, Do, and your host, Fa, hang out. We live on a **staff**. It has five lines and four spaces. Each line and space has a letter.

Our quarter-note personalities have taken their places on the staff. The order in which they line up is called the **scale**.

Music is written in many different **key signatures** like the keys of G, D, and A. The key signature for this scale is C. In the **Key of C**, Do starts the scale on the C line below the staff.

Musical Friends

We couldn't make music without our friends. **G Clef** is a tall, curly chap. He appears first on the **staff**.

Sharp looks like tic-tac-toe. He is sometimes found next to G clef, either by himself or with some of his brothers.

Flat looks like a backwards half note. Like Sharp, she is sometimes found next to G Clef either by herself or with some of her sisters or brothers.

Time Signature is the acrobat of the staff. 4/4, 3/4, and 2/4 are some of his popular cousins.

The Staff Is Like a Hotel

Let's pretend the staff is a hotel where music is made. The notes are the guests, and their musical friends are the workers.

G Clef is the doorman. He welcomes the notes. **Time Signature** is the desk clerk. He tells the notes how many beats of music they can make in each room. Each room is called a **Measure**.

Sharp and **Flat** are the bellboys. They take the notes to their rooms and place them on a line or space. Each line and space has its own letter—C, D, E, F, G, A, B, C. As you can see, the notes have put on their special faces and the music begins.

Making music is like solving an arithmetic problem. The time signature for our hotel is 4/4. That means the notes that occupy each of the hotel's three rooms must add up to four beats.

The first room has two quarter notes (1 beat each) and one half note (2 beats).

$$1 + 1 + 2 = 4$$

The second room has a dotted half note (3 beats) and two eighth notes (½ beat each).

$$3 + ½ + ½ = 4$$

The third room has one whole note (4 beats).

$$4 = 4$$

Now wasn't that easy?

The Notes and Their Beats

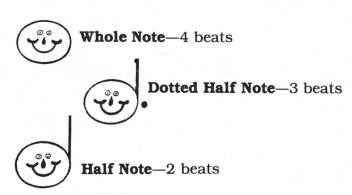

Whole Note—4 beats

Dotted Half Note—3 beats

Half Note—2 beats

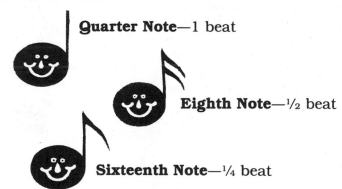

Quarter Note—1 beat

Eighth Note—½ beat

Sixteenth Note—¼ beat

*In the United Kingdom these familiar notes have different names: **semibreve** (whole note), **dotted minim** (dotted half note), **minim** (half note), **crotchet** (quarter note), **quaver** (eighth note), **semiquaver** (sixteenth note).*

61

Compose a Song

 "Mary Had a Little Lamb" is a popular song that's written mostly in quarter notes. The song has a title and two staffs, each with its own G clef. Can you find the half notes and the whole note? Add up the beats of the notes in each measure of "Mary Had a Little Lamb." Did you discover that each measure has four beats? If you did, you are on your way to becoming a composer.

Sheet music is the written record of a song. Now that you have learned all about the staff, notes, and their friends, you are ready to write your own music. When you finish your **composition**, ask someone who reads music, like a school teacher, neighbor, brother, or sister, to play your tune.

MARY HAD A LITTLE LAMB

Sheet Music

Here's how you can make your own sheet music. If you want, you can also write words to your own song. Composers write songs and they also write music without words.

Things You Need
2 sheets of white paper
cellophane tape • ruler
crayons or markers

1. Tape two sheets of paper together along the length. Fold them in half along the taped side.

2. For the cover, draw the title of your song, your name, and a picture that fits the song. Use crayons or markers.
3. Open the taped papers.
4. Write the title of your song and your name on the top of the left paper.
5. Draw a staff with five lines with G clefs on both papers. Divide each staff into three measures. Draw 4/4 on the first staff.
6. In each measure, draw different notes that add up to four beats.

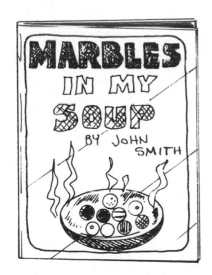

Staff Hotel Organizer

 This organizer is a great place to store your music projects. You could also use this storage box for comic books, homework assignments, and test papers. Check these important things into the Staff Hotel Organizer so you will know where to find them when you need them.

Things You Need

large cereal box • scissors
colored paper
markers or crayons • paste

1. Cut away the opened side of an empty cereal box (a).

2. Cut colored paper to fit on all sides of the box.
3. Using crayons and markers, draw a staff, G Clef, the Note family, and friends on the paper for the front of the organizer (b). Add flowers and bushes.
4. Draw bricks, bushes, flowers, and

windows on the back and side papers.
5. Paste the papers to the box (c).
6. For a roof, fold a piece of colored paper in half along the length. Draw a shingle design (d).
7. Make a sign for the roof that says "STAFF HOTEL" (e).
8. Paste the sign on the roof (f).
9. Rest the roof on top of the box.

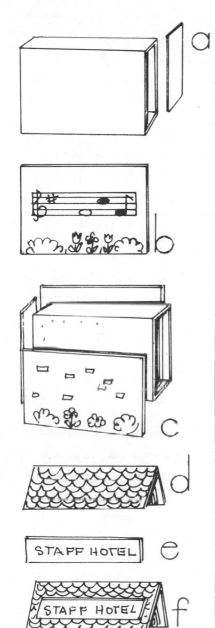

Music Stand

When musicians play in a band or an orchestra, they cannot hold their instruments and their sheet music at the same time. That's why they place their sheet music on music stands.

Now that you've started writing music, you'll also need your own music stand. When you are not performing for your friends or family, use the stand to show off a favorite original song or a colorful art project.

Things You Need

poster board • ruler • pencil
scissors • masking tape
paper towel tubes • tape
large juice can
plaster of Paris

1. Cut a sheet of poster board in half along its length.
2. Using a ruler and a pencil, divide one of the halves of the poster board into three equal parts, leaving a small rectangle at the bottom for a tab (a). Study x, y, and z.
3. Fold along the drawn lines (b and c). Study x, y, and z.
4. Tape the tab in place (c). See the arrows.
5. Tape tubes together to form a pole (d). Make the pole as tall as you like.
6. Half fill a can with dry plaster of Paris. Slowly add water and mix (e). It should not be too stiff or too soupy. Wipe away any plaster on the outside of the can.
7. Push the pole into the center of the can (f). It should stand straight in the plaster.
8. When the plaster is hard, tape the back of the stand to the top of the pole (g).

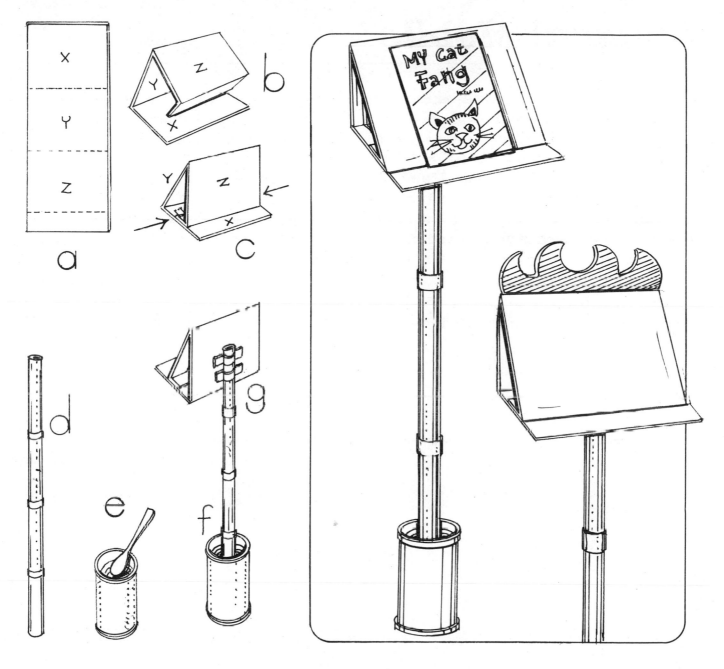

a

b

c

d

e

f

g

MY Cat Fang

Musical Mobile

 Music can be as bouncy as hip hop or as soft as a lullaby. Collect two notes, a sharp, a flat, and the G Clef to make a musical mobile. Hang it in a window and let the breezes make it swing and sway. Or let it hang peacefully in a corner of your room.

Things You Need
sturdy cardboard • ruler • pencil
scissors • colored paper • string

1. Cut cardboard into a square, about the size of this book (8 or 9 inches square).
2. Draw a sharp on the square using a ruler and pencil (a).
3. Cut out the sharp (b).
4. Make a hole in four ends with a sharpened pencil using a twisting motion (c).
5. Draw a G clef, two notes, and a flat on different colored papers (d).
6. Cut out the musical shapes (e).
7. Make a hole at the top of each shape.
8. Tie a string to each shape (f).
9. Tie the musical shapes to the holes of the sharp.
10. Tie string to the sharp and hang.

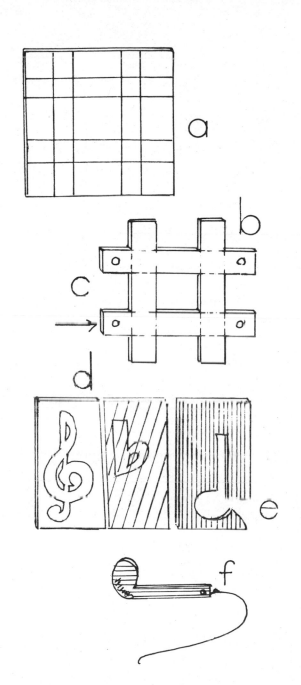

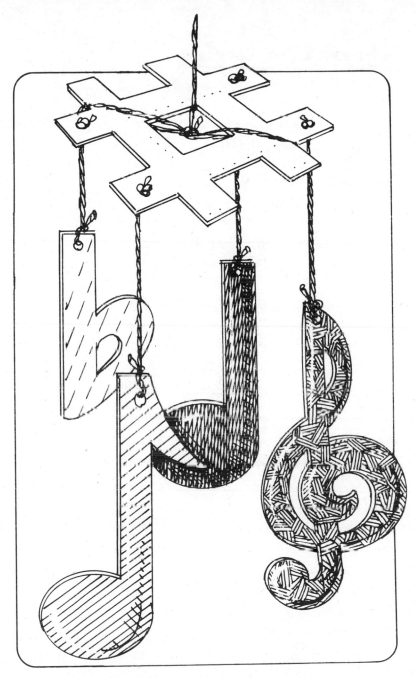

Tee Shirts

 Printed tee shirts are very popular today with both children and adults. Create your own tees with musical designs such as notes, staffs, sharps, flats, and G clef. Make one to wear in music class or give one as a present to a special friend.

Things You Need
old or new tee shirt • newspaper
permanent felt-tip markers
or fabric paints

Fold the newspaper to the size of the tee shirt. Slip it inside. Add to marker or fabric paint designs: glued-on glitter, rhinestones, iron-ons, and other decorations, if you wish.

Colorful Notes Tee

Draw colorful notes going from one shoulder down across the front and around to the back.

The Staff Tee

1. Draw the five lines of the staff. Start at one shoulder and end at the hem.
2. Add the G clef, sharps, and notes to the staff.

G Clef Tee

1. Draw a large G clef on a piece of paper until you have it just right.
2. Cut out the G clef.
3. Trace the G clef on the tee shirt with a pencil.
4. Color in the G clef.

Note Tic-Tac-Toe

 Tic-tac-toe is a favorite pencil and paper game. Here's a musical twist to this old game. Instead of the usual X's and O's, light and dark notes can be the playing pieces. The game board is a big sharp. The fun, surely, is still the same.

Things You Need
colored paper • scissors
crayons or markers

1. Cut four long strips from colored paper. They should be the same size.
2. Lay the strips on a flat surface to form a sharp.
3. Draw five notes on a dark colored paper and five on a light colored paper. They should fit inside the sharp.
4. Cut out the notes. Play the game as you would tic-tac-toe.

THE OLD JUG BAND

Born from Imagination

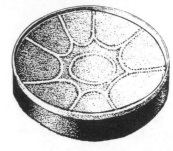

Welcome, ya'll. I'm **So**. The jug band uses musical instruments made from household items and throwaways. The band gets its name from the pottery jug that produces deep toots when someone blows into it. Although the instruments produce simple sounds, jug band music is lively and foot stomping.

Steel drums are popular in the Caribbean islands. They are made from the ends of steel barrels and played with wooden sticks.

In old times, musicians made creative musical instruments by adding round bells to wagon wheels.

Some creative people discovered that playing church bells of different sizes could make music.

Tin cans may be used many different ways in jug bands. Here is a one-string bass fiddle made from a large tin can.

When people invented drinking glasses, they discovered they could make beautiful sounds by striking them.

It's not a real jug band unless you hear a rat-tat-tat on a laundry washboard.

Another popular jug band instrument is the comb kazoo. Like a drum, it has a covering (instead of a skin or membrane) on which sounds are made.

Bottle Organ

In your home, you probably have a wonderful variety of bottles headed for recycling. Here is an easy way to recycle those bottles while adding a little "organ music" to your jug band.

Things You Need
plastic and glass bottles of different sizes

1. Arrange bottles according to size and height. Eight bottles can make a scale.
2. To play, blow into the bottles (see Cave Winds, p. 15). If you like, rearrange the bottles according to their sounds—from the lowest to the highest. To make the sound of a bottle higher, add water until you have the right note. Have an adult help you.

BOING Box

Some jug band musicians play stringed instruments made from household items, like a ham can banjo. The BOING box is another fun stringed favorite.

Things You Need
shoe box • compass • scissors
3 or 4 wide rubber bands

1. Draw a circle in the center of a shoe box cover. You can use a compass or trace around a can.
2. Cut out the circle (a). Ask an adult to help you.
3. Place the cover on the box.
4. Wrap the elastic bands around the box (b). They should all go across the hole.
5. To play this BOING box, snap the elastic bands.

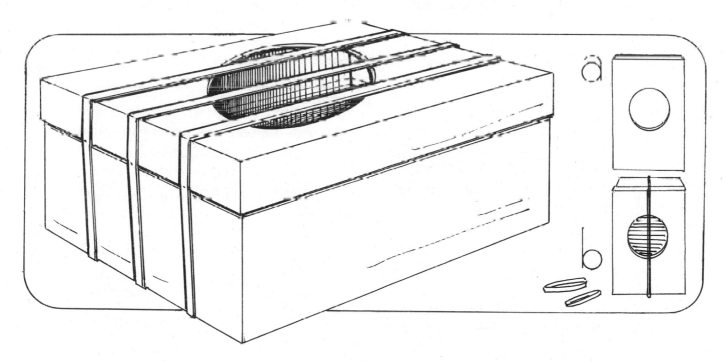

Tin Can Maracas

 Latin American music is fun to listen to. A musical instrument used to keep the beat is the *maraca*—a rattle made of wood or a dried gourd. Jug bands use maracas made from tin cans.

Things You Need
2 small cans (tomato paste)
lightweight cardboard
sharpened and unsharpened
pencils
scissors • colored paper
crayons or markers • tape
lentils, split peas, or rice
white liquid glue • ball fringe

1. Remove the tops of two small cans.
2. Have an adult punch a hole into the bottom center of each can (a). The holes should be a little smaller than the thickness of a pencil.
3. Trace around the bottom of a can on lightweight cardboard with a pencil (a). Trace two circles.
4. Cut out the circles a little away from the drawn lines (b). The cut out cir-

cles need to be a little larger than the open ends of the cans.
5. Have an adult punch a hole in the center of each circle. The holes should be a little smaller than the thickness of a pencil.
6. Cut colored paper that's as tall as each can and long enough to wrap around it.
7. Tape or glue the papers with drawn designs to the cans (c).
8. Squeeze glue around the edge of each cardboard circle (d). Place the open end of each can on the glue and dry (e).
9. Drop some lentils, split peas, or rice into the cans through a hole.
10. Push unsharpened pencils into the holes and through the cans (f). The erasers should extend beyond the cardboard circle.
11. Squeeze glue around the erasers for added strength (f). Dry.
12. Glue fringe to the bottom of the cans (g).
13. To play, hold the maracas by the handles and shake.

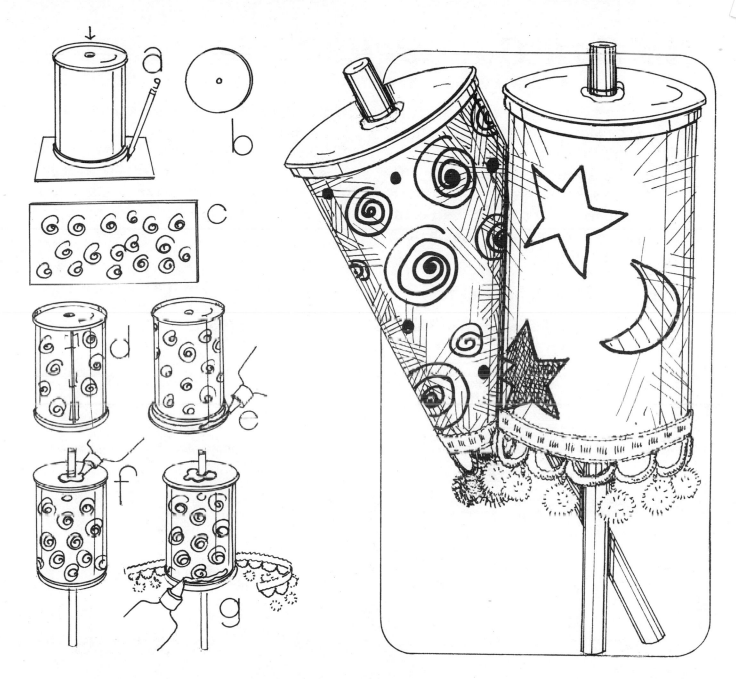

Tin Can Cow Bells

 There are two kinds of bells—clappers and pellets. The outside or inside of a **clapper bell** can be hit with a stick or metal rod, called a *clapper*. The inside of a **pellet bell** is hit with a moving ball or pellet inside. Musicians use cow bells, which have clappers. No jug band would be complete without a set of tin can cow bells.

1. Remove the lids of the opened end of the cans. Ask an adult for help.

2. Arrange all kinds of tin cans in front of you.
3. To play, hold a can and hit it with a spoon. You can also put the spoon inside the can and wave it back and forth like a clapper.

Things You Need
tin cans of different sizes
can opener
old wooden or metal spoon

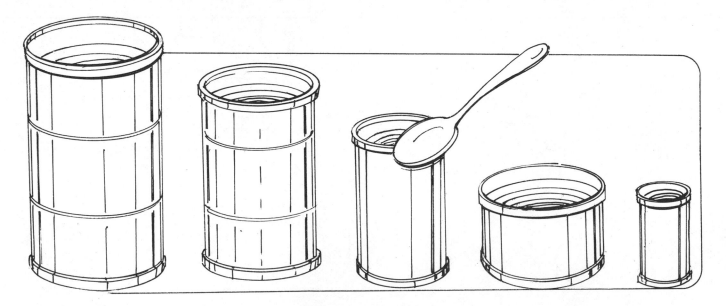

Tap-a-Taps

 In the old days, every scrap of wood left over from a building project was used. These odd pieces were turned into toys, boxes, and musical instruments. Tap-a-taps are blocks of scrap wood that you can hit together to create sounds similar to those of someone tap dancing.

1. Ask an adult to cut two pieces of scrap lumber that are a little longer than your hand. Sand the edges if you need to.

2. Ask an adult to help you screw a handle or knob on one side of each piece of wood.

3. To play, hold the tap-a-taps by the handles and hit them together. For different sounds, try hitting them gently and hard.

Things You Need
2 pieces of scrap lumber
sandpaper
2 drawer handles or knobs
2 screws • screwdriver

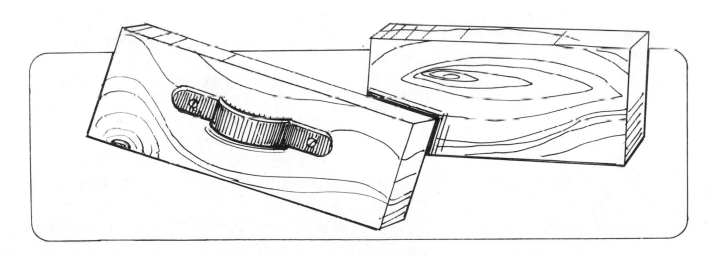

Spoon Clappers

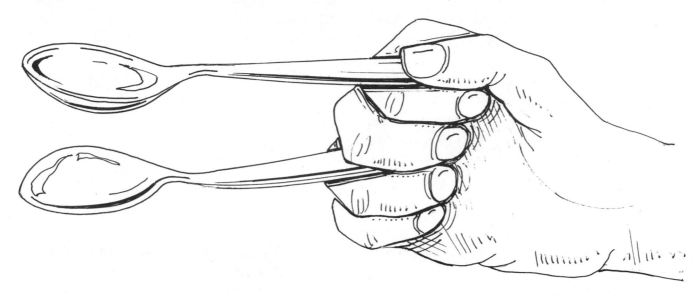

 Over 100 years ago, traveling minstrels used metal spoons as musical instruments. Some musicians played so fast that others couldn't keep up. People still play spoons today, and you must have them in a jug band!

Things You Need
2 metal spoons

1. Make a fist.
2. With the bottom facing down, place a spoon between your thumb and index finger.
3. With the bottom facing up, place a spoon between your third and fourth fingers.
4. To play, move your hand with the spoons up and down against your other hand or another part of your body, like your thigh. Keep the spoons loose. The bottoms of the spoons should easily bang against each other.

Utensil Chimes

Even cooking utensils can become musical instruments! A barbecue fork can be a harp, a ladle makes a kettle drum, and a large serving spoon turns into a bass fiddle. Add a kitchen utensil chime to a jug band, and your music will really be cooking.

Things You Need
assortment of kitchen utensils
heavy cord
lightweight cord or string
metal spoon

1. Cut a long length of heavy cord.
2. Tie kitchen utensils to the cord with lightweight cord or string. Arrange them from large to small.
3. Tie the cord between two chairs, across a doorway, or find another good place.
4. To play these chimes, hit the utensils with a spoon.

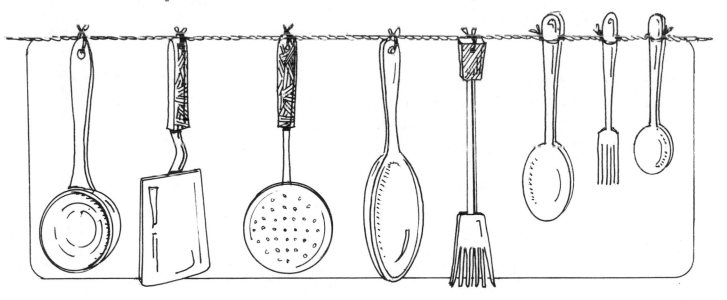

Tube Kazoo

You cannot have a jug band without a few kazoos. The tube kazoo may look like a horn, but it makes music with the voice, not the breath. Actually, kazoos belong to the drum family because they have a covering that vibrates.

Things You Need
toilet tissue or paper towel tube
waxed paper • rubber band
pencil

1. Cut from waxed paper a circle that's larger than the end of the tube. You can also use foil.
2. Place the circle centered on one end of the tube. Fold over the extra paper.
3. Attach the paper to the tube with a rubber band. The paper must be smooth and tight across the opening.
4. With a sharpened pencil, twist a hole into the tube a little way down from the paper. Ask an adult to help you.
5. To play, hold the open end of the kazoo over your mouth. Pucker your lips and sing or hum your favorite songs.

Comb Kazoo

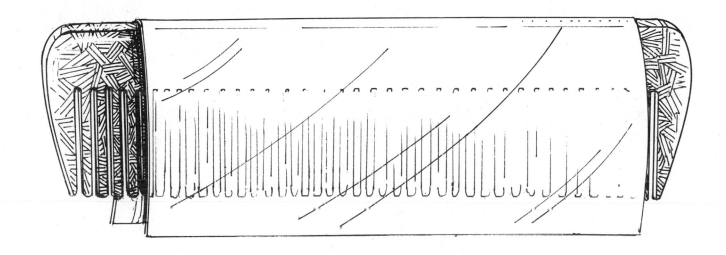

 The comb kazoo is another jug band favorite. The tube kazoo has a tight vibrating cover, but the comb kazoo's cover hangs loose. Like all kazoos, this one also needs a hum or a diddly-fiddly-do-da-da.

Things You Need
comb
piece of waxed paper or wrapping tissue paper

1. Fold a piece of waxed paper or wrapping tissue paper in half.
2. Place a comb inside the folded paper.
3. To play, hold one end of the comb. Place your lips lightly against the paper. Experiment with singing *do*'s, *da*'s, and beeps loudly and softly, high and low. The louder your voice, the more the paper will vibrate. Once you've mastered the kazoo, sing your favorite songs with words.

Knot Popper

With all the recyclable materials available today, people can create all kinds of new musical instruments for jug bands. Turn a white foam cup into a musical instrument that will make poppety-pop-pop sounds.

Things You Need
foam cup • pencil
cord or heavy string
2 metal or rubber washers

1. Cut a long length of cord.
2. Make knots along the cord. They should be close to each other (a).
3. With a sharpened pencil, make a small hole in the bottom center of a foam cup (b). It is important to make the hole just a little smaller than the knots. If the hole is too big, make a smaller hole with a large nail in another cup.
4. Feed one end of the cord through the hole.
5. Tie a washer to each end of the cord.
6. To play, pull the cord back and forth through the cup.

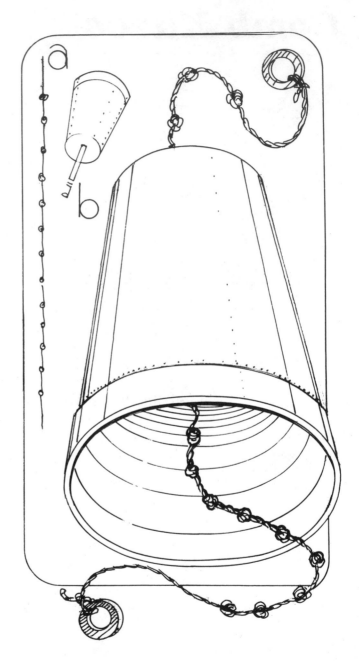

Pie Tin Cymbals

A cymbal is a round, metal musical instrument that makes a ringing sound when you hit it. When you strike *two* cymbals together, they make a crashing sound. These pie tin cymbals will be a smashing success in any jug band.

Things You Need

2 disposable aluminum pie tins
2 small drawer knobs and screws
pencil or nail

1. Make a hole in the center of two pie tins with a pencil or nail.

2. Attach a small drawer knob to the outside of each pie tin.
3. To play, hold the cymbals by the knobs and gently hit them together.

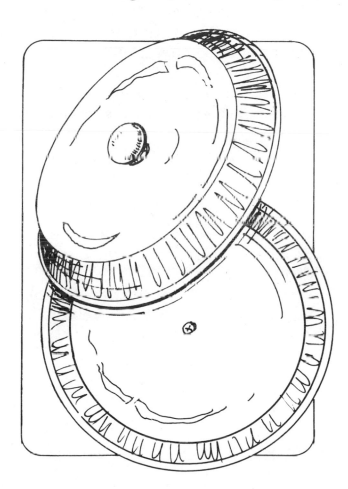

Balloon Bassoon

Here's a wind instrument for your jug band—the balloon bassoon. It makes funny sounds that often make people giggle.

Once you make all your instruments, get your band together and have a foot-stomping good time. Don't forget that when you make jug band music, my brothers and sisters will sing along.

Things You Need
balloon

1. Blow up a balloon.
2. Hold the neck of the balloon on opposite sides and stretch the neck (see arrows).
3. Let air escape. Experiment with making different sounds by stretching the neck.

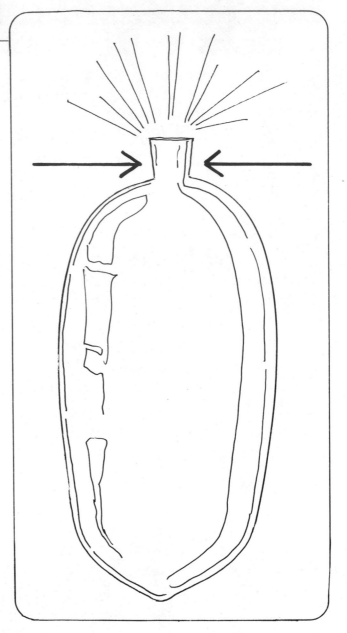

STORYBOOK MUSICIANS

Once upon a Time

La, la, la, la . . . Oh, excuse me. I'm **La**. I was just singing a scale. I'm happy to introduce you to some most famous musicians and singers who appear in legends, fairy tales, nursery rhymes, and folklore.

Angels sing in heavenly choirs. They also love to play musical instruments, especially child angels called cherubs.

In legends, sirens were beautiful women who lived on rocks in the sea. They sang so beautifully that sailors jumped into the sea to look for them.

In stories by Hans Christian Andersen and Disney, a little mermaid sings angelically.

Fairies, gnomes, and elves live in the woods. They love to dance in the moonlight and play musical instruments.

Every country has its own stories about musicians. In Greek myths, Pan is half man and half goat. He plays a flute made of reeds that's named after him, the panpipe.

Many musicians appear in nursery rhymes. "Tom, Tom, the piper's son, Learned to play when he was young. . . . Tom with his pipe did play with such skill, That those who heard him could never keep still."

Pan

 Pan, in Greek mythology, is the god of pastures, fields, and forests. This merry fellow lives in caves and loves to fish, and to frolic and dance in the woods. He is also a shepherd and a master of the panpipe. The panpipe is made of various lengths of reeds bound together.

Things You Need

paper plate • crayons or markers
colored paper • scissors
white liquid glue
brown yarn • cardboard
drinking straws

1. Draw Pan's face with crayons or markers on the underside of a paper plate.

2. Cut two horns from colored paper, and glue them to the plate above the face (a).
3. Cut brown yarn into little pieces for the hair.
4. Squeeze glue on the outer rim of the plate (b).
5. Press the yarn hair into curls in the glue.
6. To make the panpipe, cut drinking straws in different lengths, from short to long.
7. Glue the cut straws from short to long on a strip of cardboard (c).
8. On a piece of paper about as big as the plate used for Pan's face, draw Pan's curved arm (study d).
9. Glue the panpipe on Pan's mouth (e).
10. Glue Pan's arm to the back of the plate (f).

a

b

c

d

e

f

93

The Cat & the Fiddle

Hey diddle, diddle, here is a riddle. How do you get a cow to jump over the moon? Give up? Give a cat a fiddle. His lively, toe-tapping fiddling will make a cow leap.

1. Cut colored paper to fit around a can or container (a).
2. Glue or tape the paper to the can (b). The open end should be at the bottom.
3. Draw a cat's face on the can (c). Glue on broom straw whiskers.
4. Cut two pointed ears from colored paper. Glue them to the can (c).
5. Cut two long arms with rounded paws from the same colored paper. Glue or tape them to the back of the can (d).
6. Curl the arms around the can (e).
7. Fold up one paw on an angle (f).
8. Tape a drinking straw to the unfolded paw for the fiddle's bow.
9. Draw the fiddle with a pencil (see g). Add crayon or marker strings and designs. Cut out.
10. Glue the fiddle to the cat's folded paw.

Things You Need
large can or round cardboard container
colored paper • scissors
white liquid glue or tape
crayons or markers • broom straws
drinking straw • pencil

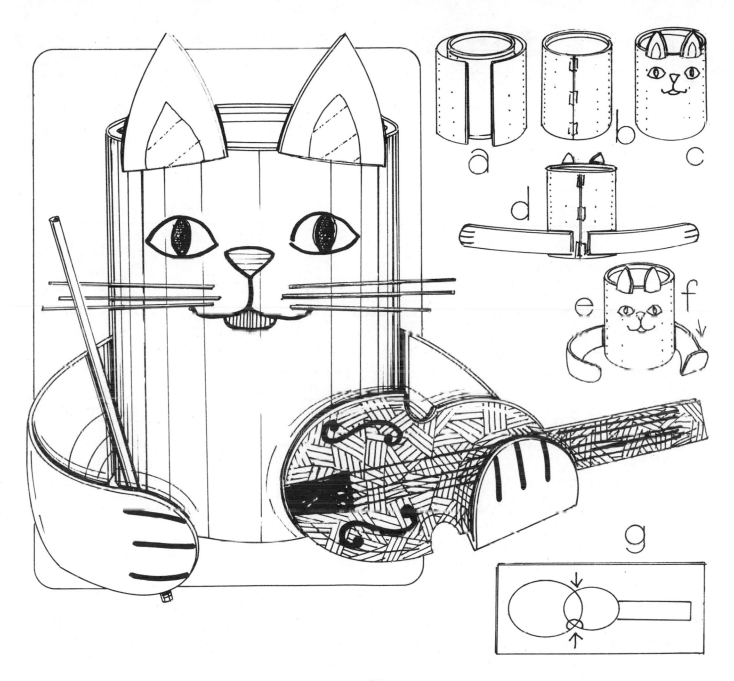

The Pied Piper

 German folktales relate the adventure of the Pied Piper. (Pied means many colors. The Pied Piper wore multi-colored clothing.) As the story goes, the town of Hamelin hired the piper to get rid of its rats. With his magical flute, he led the rats to the river, and all but one jumped in.

Things You Need
tall juice can • colored paper
scissors • tape • paste
crayons or markers
drinking straw

1. Cut red paper to wrap around a juice can. Tape or glue the paper in place (a).
2. Wrap a skin-colored strip for the head and a yellow strip for the jacket, around the can (arrows in b). Tape or glue them in place.
3. Trace the top of the can on red paper. Cut out the circle.
4. Paste the circle on top of the can (c).
5. Glue two long green paper arms to the back of the can (d).
6. On the front of the can, draw a face and buttons with crayons or markers.
7. Cut slits into strips of orange paper for the hair (e). Curl the strips.
8. Paste on the hair and a purple paper feather.
9. Curl the arms. Tape a drinking straw to one hand for the flute.
10. To make the rats, cut brown, gray, or white paper into strips of different lengths. The height of each paper should be the same.
11. Draw a rat's face and two paws in the center of each paper (f).
12. Roll each paper and tape or glue each in place.

To make all but one rat disappear, stack each inside the other, according to size.

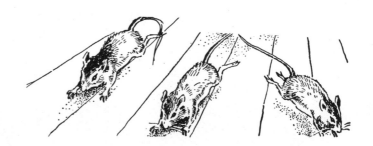

Little Boy Blue

"Little Boy Blue come blow your horn, the cow's in the meadow, the sheep's in the corn." When you lift off this Boy Blue's hat, he becomes a pencil holder or a candy box.

Things You Need

quart milk or juice carton • scissors
colored paper • tape • paste
toy horn • pencil
butter or dairy tub

1. Cut away the peak of the carton (a).
2. Cut out skin-colored paper to wrap around the carton. Tape it in place (b).
3. Cut a white paper strip for the collar that's long enough to wrap around the carton. Cut out a small V in the center (study c).
4. Wrap the collar around the carton and tape it to the back.
5. Cut slits into paper strips for the hair. Paste the strips to the top of the carton (d).
6. Paste a paper bow tie to the collar, below the V (e).
7. With crayons or markers, draw a face (f).
8. Make a hole in the carton by pushing the point of a sharpened pencil through the mouth (f).
9. Push a toy horn into the mouth.
10. For the hat, wrap colored paper around a butter tub and tape it in place (g). Cut away the extra paper around the bottom and top (h). Add a paper feather (i).
11. Place the hat on Boy Blue's head.

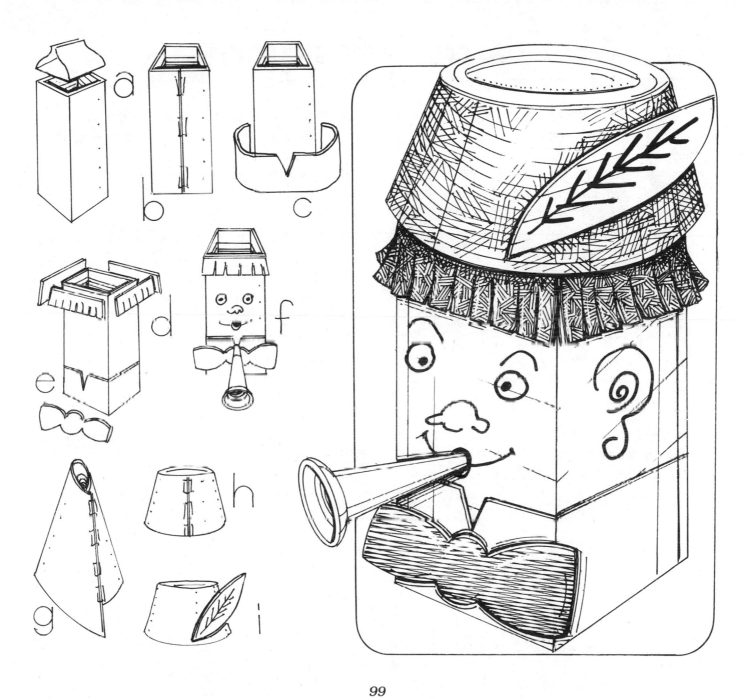

a

b

c

d

e

f

g

h

i

The Owl & the Pussycat

"The Owl and the Pussycat went to sea in a beautiful pea-green boat." In Edward Lear's poem the owl looks up at the stars and sings while he plays a small guitar. The Pussycat loves his singing and playing so much that the two marry in a year and a day.

Things You Need

milk or juice carton • scissors
colored paper • paste • stapler
small box and can • tape
crayons or markers

1. Open the peak of an empty milk or juice carton (a).
2. Cut away one side that was folded into the peak (b).
3. Cut green paper to fit on the bottom and on the two opposite sides of the carton (c).
4. Paste the papers on the carton.
5. Refold the peak and staple it closed (d) to make the boat.
6. Draw a guitar on paper. Cut it out and paste it to the side of the boat.
7. Cut colored paper to wrap around a small can and a small box. Paste or tape the paper in place (e).
8. Trace around the top of the can and the box on colored paper. Cut out and paste the paper in place.
9. The box is the owl and the can is the pussycat. Add ears, feathers, and faces with paper cutouts and crayon or marker designs.
10. Place the owl and the pussycat in the boat.

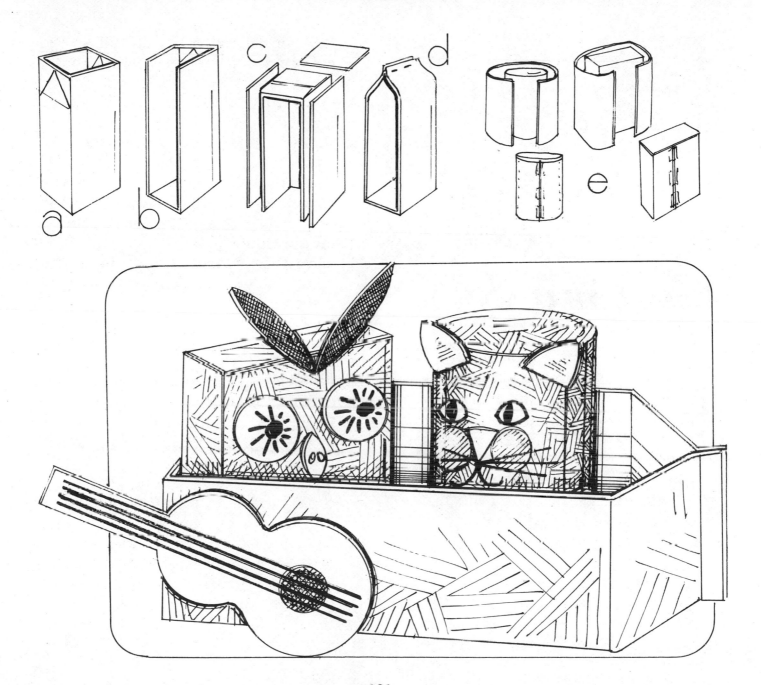

Old King Cole

"Old King Cole was a merry old soul," who liked lively tunes. He called for his pipe, bowl, and three musicians to fiddle away the afternoon. This Old King Cole and fiddlers three is a penny-toss game to keep you, like the king with his fiddlers, entertained. The clinking of pennies against the cans makes light music.

Things You Need
cans—1 large, 2 medium, 1 small
colored paper • crayons or markers
tape or paste • small dish or bowl

1. Cut out colored paper as tall as the cans and long enough to wrap around them.
2. Draw King Cole's face and hair on the largest paper (a).
3. Roll the paper around the large can. Tape or paste it in place (b).
4. Cut a strip of yellow paper for the crown. Cut out a pointy design along one long side (c). Write the number *1* on the front.
5. Wrap the crown around the top of Old King Cole's head. Tape or paste it in place (d).
6. Paste a paper pipe to Old King Cole's mouth (e).
7. Make the fiddlers the same way you did Old King Cole, but they won't have a crown or a pipe.
8. Draw and cut out a fiddle for each fiddler (see f). Write a *3* on two fiddles and a *5* on the other.
9. To play the game, each player gets an equal amount of pennies. In turn, he or she tries to toss the pennies into Old King Cole and his fiddlers three. If a penny lands in one of the characters, the player gets the number of pennies shown.

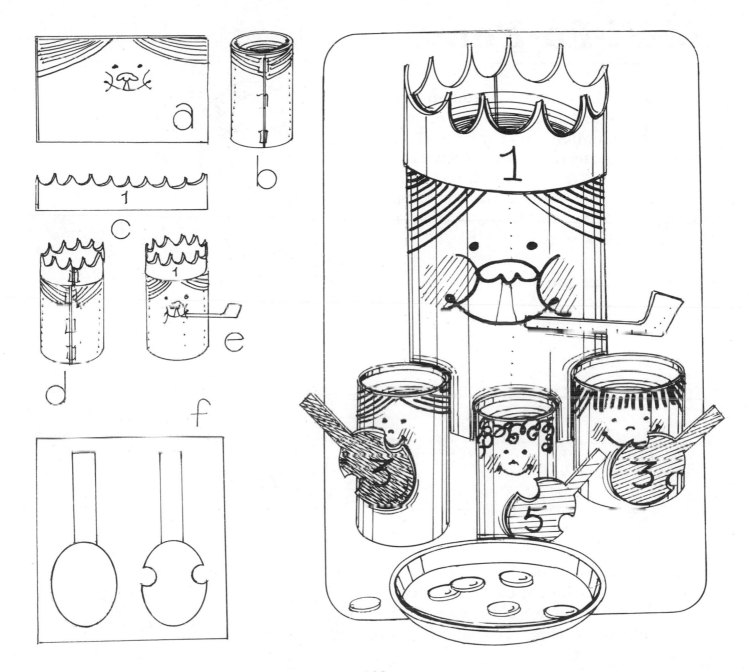

a

b

c

1

d

e

1

f

1

2

3

5

Fe-Fi-Fo-Fum

What did Jack find in the giant's castle after he climbed the beanstalk? A goose that laid golden eggs and a magical harp that could sing while it played its own strings. But you don't have to climb a beanstalk to own the giant's harp.

Things You Need
sheet of yellow poster board
pencil • crayon or markers
scissors • yardstick • paper punch
knitting yarn or cord

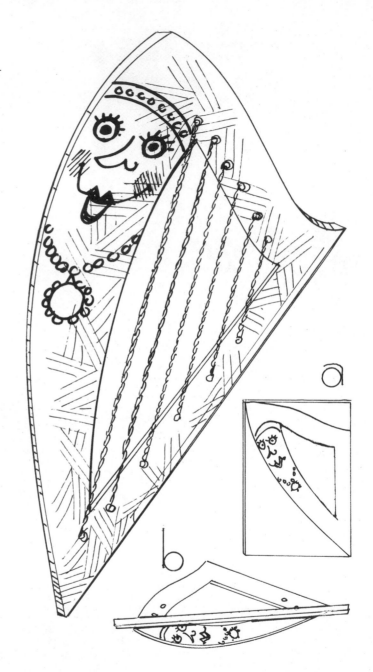

1. Draw a harp shape on a sheet of poster board (study a). Draw a face and jewelry on the long curved side.
2. Cut out the harp.
3. Using a yardstick as a guide, mark where holes will be made on two sides of the harp (b).
4. Starting at the back of the harp, weave a long yarn or cord in and out of the holes. Secure both ends with knots or paper clips.

CELEBRATION MELODIES

Let the Party Begin

Christmas is celebrated in many countries. Plum pudding comes from England, the Christmas tree is from Germany, and the Nativity crèche comes from Italy.

Music makes Christmas merry. Church bells ring and carolers sing. The angel chime is a popular music maker. Angels strike bells as they spin from the heat of burning candles.

 I'm **Ti**. This is my favorite chapter because it's all about celebrations. Travel the world with me to see how people celebrate special holidays with music, song, and dance.

St. Patrick's Day honors the patron saint of Ireland. This is a day when leprechauns play horns and dance jigs. Catch one by its coattails, and your wish will come true.

Carnival is celebrated in Latin American countries for three days before Ash Wednesday and the beginning of Lent. Carnival has lots of singing, dancing, costumes, and parades.

Chinese people around the world celebrate their New Year sometime between the end of January to the beginning of March. During Chinese New Year's a large dragon dances down the streets and goes from door to door. Of course, the dragon is really a long costume with people inside who make it dance.

During the cherry viewing festivals in Japan, families gather for a picnic under the blooming cherry trees. After a meal, everyone joins the dancing and singing.

New Year's Eve Horn

Welcoming in the new year by blowing horns and banging pots is fun! This New Year's Eve, double your noisy celebration with this giant horn.

Things You Need

party horn • colored paper
crayons or markers • tape
scissors • rubber band

1. Draw designs on a sheet of colored paper with crayons or markers.
2. Wrap the paper tightly around a horn (a). The mouthpiece should extend beyond the paper.
3. Tape the paper in place (b).
4. Cut the bottom of the paper so that it's even.
5. If the paper slips off the horn, keep it in place with rubber band near the mouthpiece.

Chinese New Year Gong

Every Chinese year celebrates an animal, like the year of the horse or the year of the dog. During Chinese New Year festivities, someone strikes a large gong to noisily announce the arrival of the dancing dragon.

Things You Need
disposable pie tin • large cereal box
tape • red paper • scissors • paste
pencil • ruler • cord • cork
paper clip

1. Tape the opened end of a cereal box closed.
2. Trace the front, sides, and top of the box on red paper (a). Cut them out.
3. Paste the papers on the box.
4. Draw a window on the front of the box with a pencil and ruler (b). Cut out.
5. Ask an adult to make a hole in the side of the pie tin and in the center of the top of the box (c).
6. Tie a long cord to the pie tin (d).
7. To hang the gong, push the cord through the hole inside of the box (e).

The underside of the pie tin should face out. Tie the cord to a paper clip.
8. Make the padded beater out of a pencil pushed into a cork.

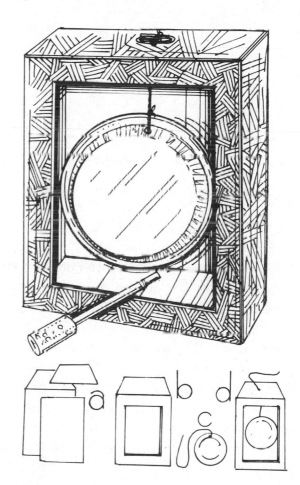

Lute Valentine

Young men once stood under their sweetheart's window to play and sing love songs. About 400 years ago, they played a stringed instru- ment with a bent neck, called a lute. This heart-shaped lute is a Valentine card any special friend will love to receive.

Things You Need

red and white paper • scissors
paste • crayons or markers

1. Cut out a long heart from white paper. Cut a scalloped design into the edge of the heart (a).
2. Cut a second heart from red paper, smaller than the white heart. Cut out a small white circle and paste it on the red heart (b).
3. Paste the red heart on the white heart (c).
4. Cut a long strip of red paper for the lute's neck. Paste one end to the heart (d). Fold over the other end (e).
5. Paste small white hearts to the folded end.

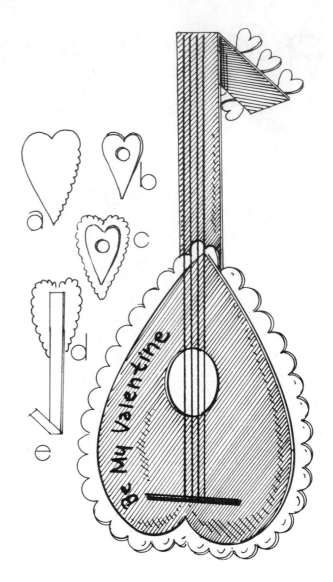

6. Draw the strings, a bar, and a Val- entine message on the lute with cray- ons or markers.

St. Pat's Harp

Harps accompany Irish ballads. They have been popular in Ireland for hundreds of years. This harp with green strings promises the "luck of the Irish" to all who rub its shamrock. This one won't make music, but it's fun.

Things You Need

white poster board
pencil • scissors
green paper • paste
paper punch • green knitting yarn
tape

1. Draw a harp shape on a large square of poster board (study a). Cut it out.
2. Cut a bar long enough to lay across the top of the harp (b).
3. Paste the bar to the top of the harp (c).
4. Cut out a shamrock from green paper. Paste it to the bottom of the harp.
5. With a paper punch, punch an equal number of holes into the bar and into the bottom of the harp (d). Ask an adult for help.

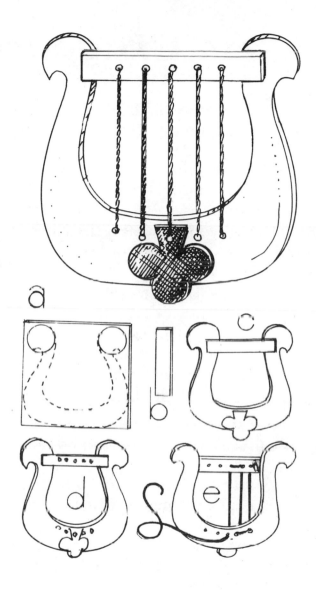

6. Weave a long green yarn in and out of the holes, at the back of the harp (e). Tape the ends in place.

Purim Gragger

Purim is the happiest and noisiest Jewish holiday. Whenever someone says the name *Haman*, children stomp their feet and whirl their noisemakers called graggers. Graggers are really folk musical instruments from Europe called cog rattles.

Things You Need
small candy or caramel
popcorn box
rice or dried beans • tape • pencil
drinking straw • ribbon
2 rubber bands

1. Add a little rice or dried beans to a small box. Tape the open end closed (a).
2. Carefully twist the point of a sharpened pencil through the box near the taped end (b).
3. Push an end of a drinking straw through the holes (c). The longer end will be the handle.
4. Tie ribbon to the straw at each hole (c).
5. Completely wrap a rubber band around the straw at each end (d). Push the rubber bands up to the ribbons. The box should spin freely.

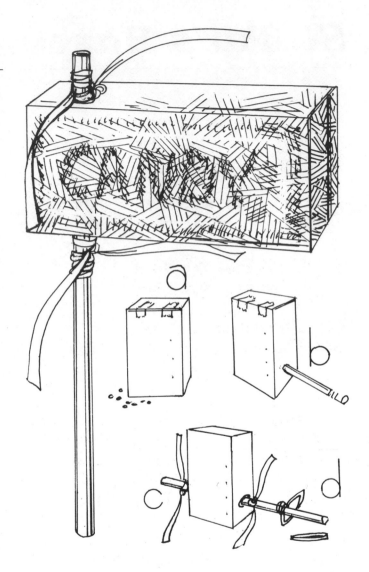

Halloween Clatter Stick

In England, on Guy Fawkes Day (November 5) children dress in costumes and beg, "A penny for the old Guy." In Canada and the United States on October 31, children in costumes shout, "Trick or treat" for Halloween. Next Halloween or Guy Fawkes Day, take a clatter stick along to scare away the ghosts, goblins, black cats, and witches.

Things You Need
cork • sharpened pencil
unsharpened pencil
metal washers • jingle bells
string • heavy tape
white liquid glue

1. Twist a sharpened pencil into a cork to make a hole (a).
2. Squeeze glue into the hole (b).
3. Push the end of an unsharpened pencil into the hole (c). Let the glue dry.
4. Slip metal washers onto the pencil. Also tie on jingle bells in twos and threes.
5. Wrap enough tape around the pencil

so that the washers and bells don't slip off the end. But make sure there's enough space between the washers and bells so they can hit each other when you shake the stick.

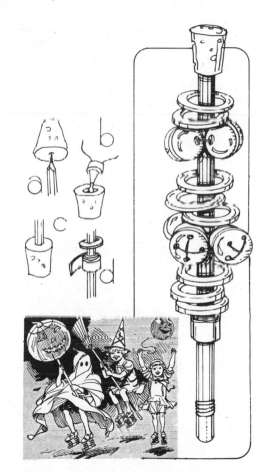

Christmas Bells

Christmas is the season of silver bells, sleigh bells, and church bells. Someone said, every time a bell rings, an angel receives its wings. Here are two bell door hangings that will jingle a welcome to holiday guests.

Things You Need

ribbon • red, white, or green felt
large and small jingle bells
needle and thread
safety pin
knitting yarn or string
foam cups • pencil
pipe cleaner • poster board
scissors • paper punch

Sleigh Bell Pull

1. Cut a strip of felt for the bell pull.
2. Sew large jingle bells to the strip. Ask an adult to help you.
3. Attach a large ribbon bow to the top of the bell pull with a safety pin. The pin should be at the back.
4. Tie a piece of yarn or string to the safety pin for hanging (a).

Church Bell Spray

1. Make a hole in the bottom of a foam cup, using the point of a pencil (b). Center the hole.
2. Attach the end of a pipe cleaner to a small jingle bell (c).
3. Make a knot in the pipe cleaner a little down from the end (d).
4. Push the end of the pipe cleaner into the cup and out the hole. Twist the end into a loop (e).
5. Tie different lengths of string or yarn to the loops of several bells.
6. Cut out a large poster board bow. Punch holes along the bottom edge.
7. Tie the bells to the holes.
8. Tie yarn to the bow and hang.

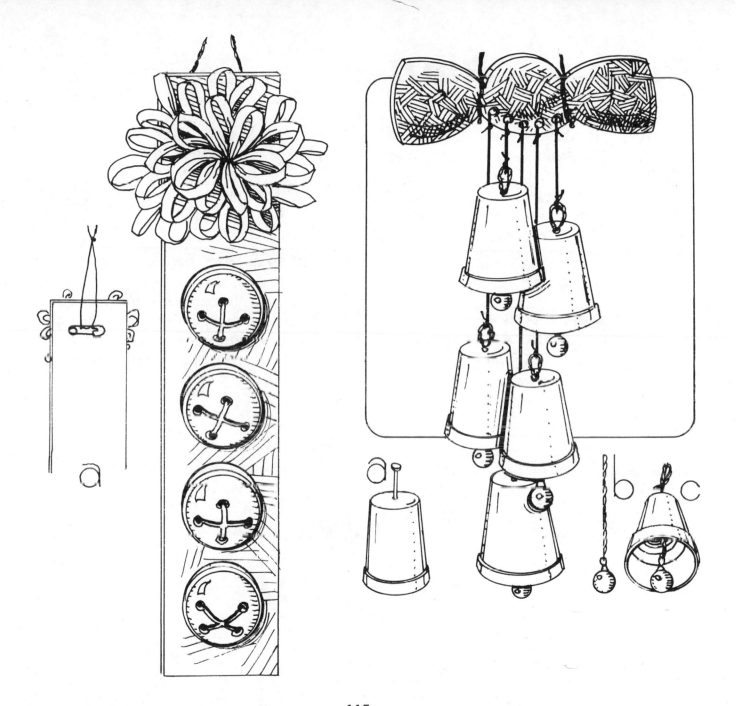

Birthday Rattler

Birthdays are popular celebrations because everybody has one! Make your party complete with your family and friends singing "Happy Birthday to You" to the clatter of these noisemakers.

Things You Need
2 paper plates • dried beans or rice
white liquid glue
crayons or markers

1. Put some dried beans or rice on a paper plate (a).
2. Squeeze glue around the rim (b).
3. Place another plate on top of the glued plate, rim to rim (c). Dry.
4. Decorate the plates with birthday designs.

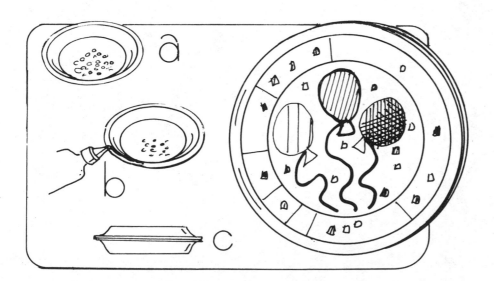

SING A HAPPY SONG

Tickle Your Vocal Cords

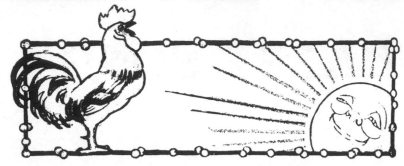

Remember me? I'm **Do**, Do's twin. I sing a little higher than him. And singing is what this chapter is all about. We live in a world filled with songs, from the rooster's cock-a-doodle-doo in the morning to the crickets' chirping when the sun goes down.

In Greek tales, Odysseus heard the Sirens sing. His sailors put wax in their ears and strapped Odysseus to the mast of their ship to keep them all from jumping overboard.

Ancient Egyptians not only played harps and horns, but they sang beautiful songs to their kings, called pharaohs.

During the Christmas season in merry old England, the sounds of carolers fill the air.

When the phonograph was invented, it felt like having a singer in the living room. The first records were wax cylinders that made voices sound high.

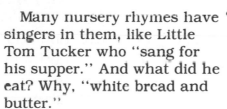

Many nursery rhymes have singers in them, like Little Tom Tucker who "sang for his supper." And what did he eat? Why, "white bread and butter."

Singers also appear in story books. In Lewis Carroll's "Alice in Wonderland," Alice visits the Duchess, who sings a lullaby to her "child."

Of course, every child's mother sings the most special lullaby of all.

Singing Cowboy & Cowgirl

In the early days of the American West, cowboys tended cattle on ranches. At night, over campfires, they sang songs about life on the range. If you enjoy listening to country/western music, stand these cowpokes beside the radio.

Things You Need

2 toilet paper tubes • colored paper
scissors • crayons or markers
paste or tape

1. Cut brown paper to wrap around two toilet paper tubes. Paste or tape the paper in place (a).
2. Cut a skin-colored strip of paper for each face. Paste or tape the strips around the tops of the tubes (b).
3. Draw a face for the cowboy and the cowgirl on the tubes with markers.
4. For the cowgirl's skirt, cut a piece of brown paper long enough to wrap around the tube. Cut slits into the bottom edge (c).
5. Paste or tape the skirt in place (d). It should flair out a little at the bottom.
6. For the cowgirl's jacket, cut a strip of brown paper that almost wraps around the tube. Cut slits into the bottom edge (e).
7. Paste or tape the jacket below the face (f).
8. For the cowboy, paste or tape on a jacket. Also add two paper strips with slits for the pants or chaps (g).
9. Cut out two arms for both the cowboy and cowgirl. Cut slits along the bottom edge.
10. Paste or tape the arms to the back of the jackets (h).

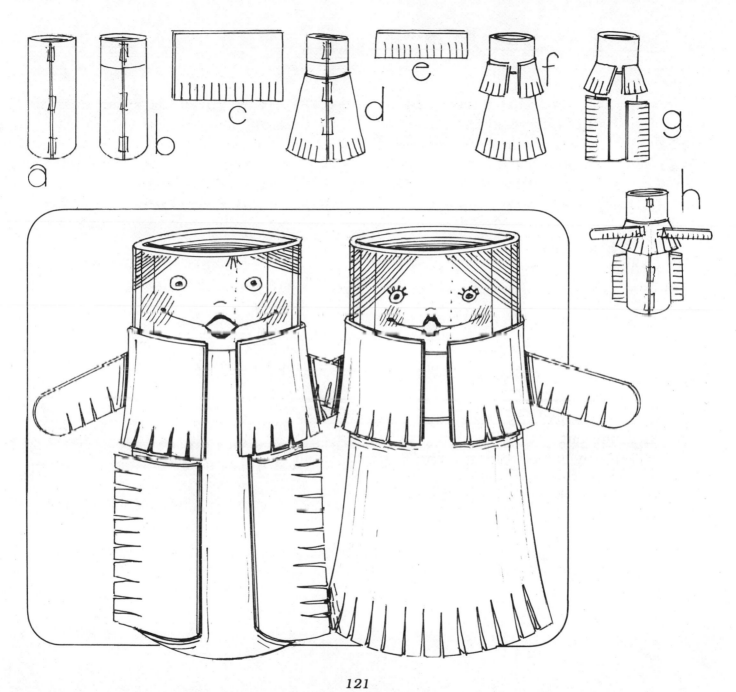

The Little Mermaid

 The little mermaid in Hans Christian Andersen's story gave up something very precious to become a real girl— her beautiful singing voice. But the story has a happy ending.

Things You Need

colored paper • pencil • scissors
empty medium and small can
paste • tape
very small paper cup
cardboard • yarn

1. Draw a fishtail on green paper (a). Cut it out.
2. Draw many ovals on green paper (b). Cut them out.
3. Paste a row of ovals around the bottom of a medium-size can. The closed end of the can should be at the top (c). Cover the can with rows of ovals. Overlap each row.
4. Paste the fishtail to the can near the bottom (d).
5. Cut out skin-colored paper to wrap around the small can. Paste or tape the paper in place (e).
6. Cut out two arms from skin-colored paper. Paste them to the back of the can (f).
7. Wrap skin-colored paper around a small cup. Paste or tape them in place (g).
8. Cut away the extra paper at the top and bottom of the cup (h).
9. To make the hair, wrap yarn around a piece of cardboard. Tie the yarn together at one end (i). Cut through the yarn at the opposite end (j).
10. Draw a face on the cup.
11. Glue the hair to the top of the cup (k).
12. Place the head on the body and the body on the tail.

Chorus of Angels

One singing angel is a solo. Two is a duet. Three is a trio. Four is a quartet. What do you call fifty singing angels? Why, a heavenly chorus, of course.

Things You Need

2 white foam cups • scissors
markers • white liquid glue
colored paper • paste
small paper doily
ball fringe or cotton balls

First Angel

1. Cut away most of the open end of a foam cup for the angel's head.
2. Draw a face on the head with markers (a).
3. Glue the bottom of the head to the bottom of another foam cup (b).
4. Cut a long strip of white paper for the arms. Round the ends.

5. Paste the arms to the bottom cup (c).
6. Cut two wings from white paper. Paste them over the arms (d).
7. Curl the arms to the front of the cup. Paste a folded paper songbook to the hands (e).
8. Place a yellow circle on the head for a halo.

Second Angel

1. Cut a circle out of the center of a small doily (a). The hole should be large enough to fit over the bottom of a foam cup.
2. Push the bottom of the cup through the hole in the doily (b). Press the doily against the cup to form the dress.
3. Draw on a face with markers.
4. The hair can be either cotton balls or balls cut from ball fringe. Glue the balls to the angel's head (c).
5. Paste on arms and wings.

Singing Hands

 Most puppets have heads the puppeteer moves with his hands. But did you know that some puppets have heads that are actually hands? Although these two heads don't have bodies, they can sing along with your favorite songs.

Things You Need

2 hands • watercolor markers
yarn • tape

1. Make the hair from tied pieces of yarn. Braid the girl's hair.
2. Make your hand into a fist. Draw a mouth and eyes on the thumb and index finger for the boy. Also do this on the other fist for the girl.
3. Tape hair to each hand.
4. To make your hands sing, move your thumbs up and down.

Singing Noids

Noids have no noses. But they do have large mouths for singing. Create a collection of people, animal, and vegetable noids and have a singing good time.

Things You Need
sheet of white or
light colored paper
crayons or markers • pencil
paper punch • scissors
ribbon or string

1. Draw eyes on a long side of a sheet of paper (a). They should be centered near the bottom edge of the paper. Draw hair above the eyes.
2. Punch a hole into the two short sides of the paper (see arrows in b).
3. To draw eye holes, place the paper on your face with the noid's eyes just above your mouth. Lightly mark where your eyes fall with a pencil.
4. Cut out eye holes large enough to see through.
5. Tie ribbon or string into each hole (c).
6. Wrap the paper around your face with the bottom edge just below your nose. Tie the noid mask in place.
7. Look in a mirror to see a noid sing.

Human Jukebox

A human jukebox does not work with records and electricity. When you drop a coin into the slot, the door opens, and the singer inside sings a request. Ask an adult to help you with this project.

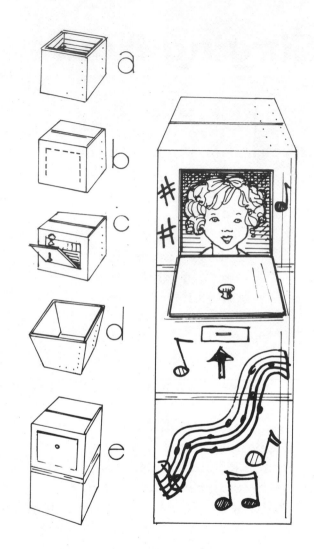

Things You Need

corrugated cardboard cartons of the same size (taller than you are when they're stacked)
knife • strong tape • paints
paintbrush • small knob

1. Cut away the opened flaps of a carton (a). This will be the top of the jukebox.
2. Cut three sides of a door into the front side (dotted lines in b).
3. Fold the door out and screw a small knob on the inside of the door (c).
4. Cut out a window for air on one side of each carton.
5. Cut away the tops and bottoms of the other cartons (d).
6. Tape all the cartons together. The door should face the front and the windows should be at the back (f).
7. Paint the jukebox. Add musical designs.
8. Cut out a coin slot below the door.

Practice Microphone

The next time you belt out a song, this play microphone will help get you into the groove.

Things You Need
toilet tissue tube • black paper tape • foam ball • white liquid glue small paper cup

1. Tape black paper around a tube (a).
2. Rest a foam ball in a small cup.
3. Place the tube on top of the ball.

4. Squeeze a lot of glue around the tube where it touches the ball (b). Let it dry.

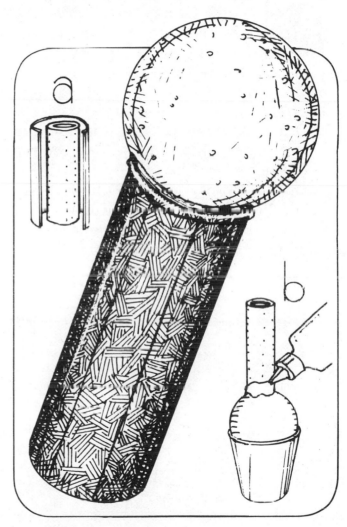

Blackbirds in a Pie Game

 In the nursery rhyme "Sing a Song of Sixpence," four and twenty blackbirds are baked in a pie. The blackbirds sing as soon as the pie is opened. If blackbird pie sounds tasty to you, cook one up for this fun game.

1. Draw air holes on the underside of one paper plate. This will be the top of the pie.
2. Cut out twenty-four blackbirds. They can be very simple in shape.
3. Place the blackbirds inside a second plate.
4. Place the plate with the air holes over the plate with the blackbirds.
5. Each player rolls a die to see how many blackbirds he or she can take. If the player forgets to sing "May I?" before removing the birds, the birds must stay in the pie. The winner has the most birds when the pie is empty.

Things You Need
2 plain paper plates
crayons or markers
black paper • scissors • die

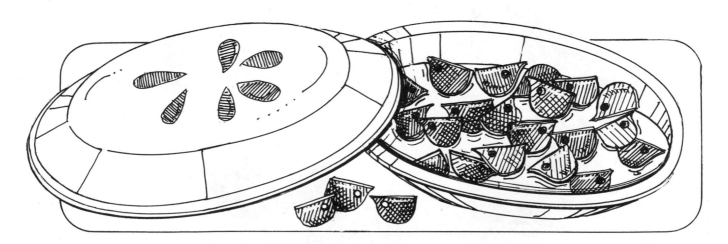

DANCE,

DANCE,

DANCE

Music for Your Feet

It's great to see you. I'm **Flat**. People have moved their feet to music since the very beginning. They waltz in ballrooms, jig on stage, and in "The Twelve Days of Christmas," nine ladies dance.

In ancient Egypt, young girls danced with balls tied to their hair. The balls swung with the movement of the dance.

Every country has its own dances. In some European countries, people wear colorful costumes in traditional dances. Some Native Americans meet at powwows to compete in dancing.

At Halloween, we're told, goblins, black cats, witches, and ghosts dance in the moonlight.

In European folklore, elves and fairies who live in forests also dance at night when they can't be seen. But they leave fairy rings on the grass.

Dancing plays a part in many children's games, like "Ring around the Rosey," "London Bridge," and musical chairs.

In Lewis Carroll's "Alice in Wonderland," Alice meets the Gryphon and the Mock Turtle, who ask, "Will you, won't you, will you, won't you, will you join the dance?"

Maypole

People around the world celebrate spring with a May Day festival. Sometimes they set up a maypole in the center of town. They decorate the maypole with long ribbons or crêpe paper streamers and spring flowers. Grab a ribbon or streamer and dance and sing around your own maypole.

Things You Need
7 or more cans of the same size
sewing thread spool • glue
sharpened pencil
unsharpened pencil • paper plate
rolls of crêpe paper streamers
scissors • paper clip • strong tape
plaster of Paris • small bucket
stirring stick

1. Glue an empty sewing spool on the middle of the closed end of a can (a). Insert a pencil into the hole.

2. Make a hole in the middle of a paper plate, and six holes equally spaced around the rim (b).
3. Cut crêpe paper streamers as long as the maypole will stand.
4. Tie the end of each streamer to a paper clip (c).
5. Attach the paper clips to the holes on the rim of the plate (d).
6. Tape cans together to form a pole (e). The spool is at the top. The open end of the bottom faces out.
7. Mix plaster of Paris in a small bucket.
8. Push the pole into the plaster (f). It should stand up straight.
9. When the plaster is hard, decorate the pole with crêpe paper streamers and paper flowers (g).
10. Rest the plate over the pencil on the top can (h). The plate should spin freely.

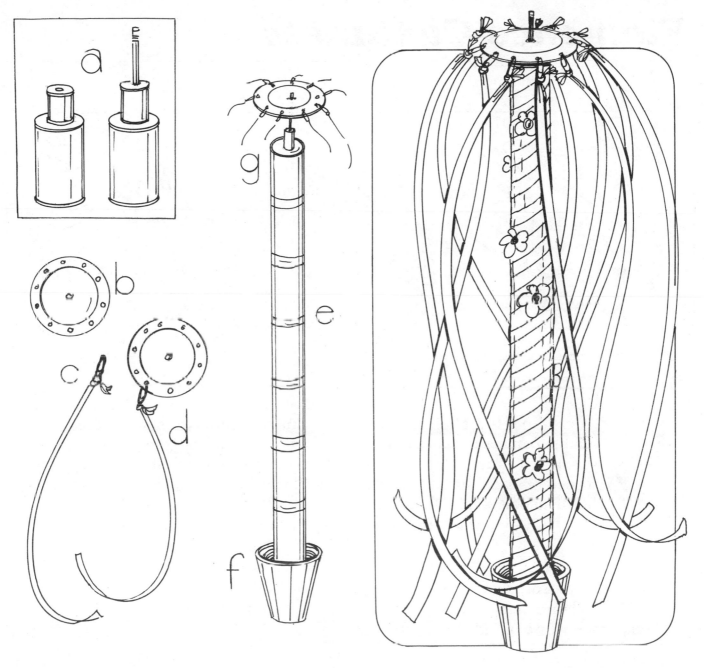

Flamenco Castanets

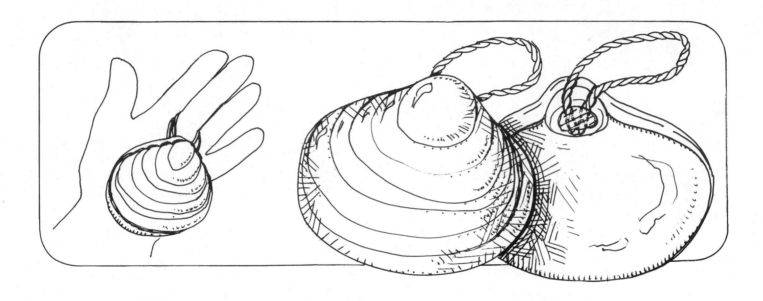

A castanet is a shell-shaped clapper made of hard wood. Usually a dancer plays a castanet in each hand. Gypsy flamenco dancers in Spain dress in bright, frilly costumes and play the castanets.

Things You Need

2 clean clam shells • cord
scissors • white liquid glue

1. Cut cord into two short pieces.
2. Squeeze a lot of glue on the inside of two washed clam shells, at the top.
3. Place the ends of each piece of cord into the glue. Dry.
4. To play, slip the loops onto your middle finger. They should hang loose. Tap the clam shells with your fingers so that they hit each other to make clicking sounds.

Powwow Bells

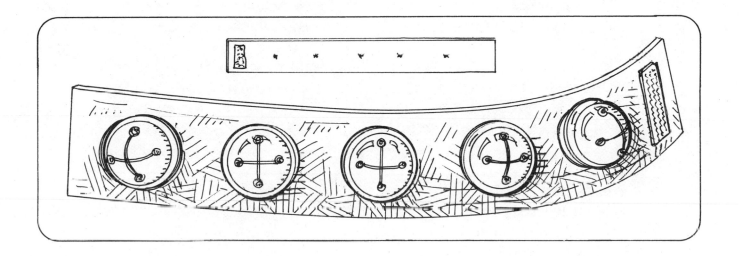

bNative Americans wear bands of jingle bells around their wrists and ankles when they perform traditional dances. With every step the dancers take, the bells jingle.

Things You Need
felt • jingle bells
needle and thread
self-fastening tape (Velcro)

1. Cut a band from felt long enough to wrap around your ankle or wrist, plus a little extra.
2. Sew on jingle bells along the band with a needle and thread. Ask an adult to help you.
3. Sew self-fastening tape to overlapping ends of the band. Ask an adult for help.

Tinikling Poles

Tinikling poles are from the Philippine Islands. The sounds of long bamboo poles hitting wood blocks create the beat for dancers. The tinikling folk dance represents the long-legged crane wading in water and wind-blown reeds.

1. Two pole movers kneel on the floor with a block of wood in front of each.
2. A dancer steps in and out of the space created when the pole movers shift the poles on and off the blocks. Experiment to make your own dance steps.

Things You Need
2 long poles (closet poles, broomsticks, or dowels)
2 blocks of wood

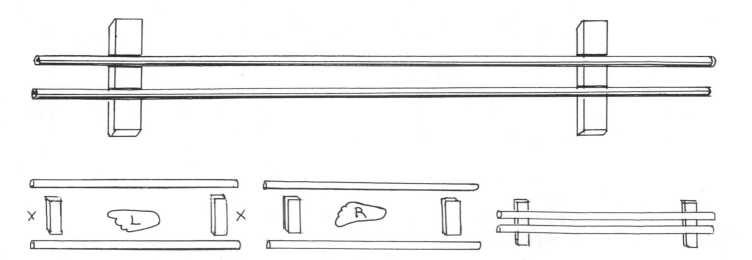

Limbo Pole

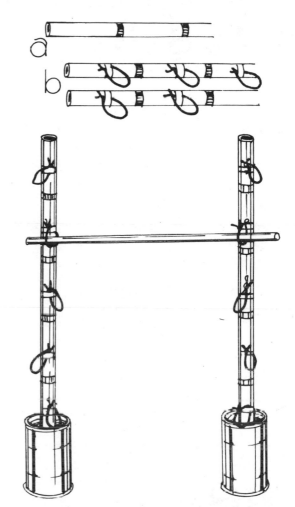

A favorite Caribbean dance is the limbo. Dancers pass under a limbo pole. As the limbo pole is lowered, the dancers have to bend backwards to pass under it. As your next party, set up a limbo pole and see how low your friends can go.

Things You Need
cardboard tubes • strong tape
cord • scissors • 2 large juice cans
plaster of Paris • stirring stick
broom handle

1. Tape cardboard tubes together into two poles (a). They should be the same length.
2. Cut many pieces of cord as long as this book. Knot each cord into a loop. The loops should be big enough for a broom handle to pass through.
3. Lay the poles on the floor side by side.
4. Tape loops along both poles. The loops on each pole should be side by side those of the opposite pole (b).
5. For each pole, mix plaster of Paris in a can with a stirring stick. Fill it al-most to the top. Ask an adult for help. Push a pole into the middle of the can. Be sure it stands straight.
6. When the plaster hardens, stand the poles a distance from each other. Slip a broom handle into loops opposite each other on the vertical poles.

Hula Skirt

In Hawaii, a traditional dance is the popular hula. Dancers wear grass skirts and chains of flowers called leis. The dancers speak the stories of the songs with their hands, as they sway in grass skirts. Musicians play ukuleles, which are small guitars.

Things You Need

package of crêpe paper • scissors
stapler • ribbon

1. Cut crêpe paper that's long enough to wrap around your waist.

2. Fold a little of the top edge of the crêpe paper twice to form a waistband. Staple it in place (a).
3. Cut slits into the crêpe paper along the bottom length (b). Don't cut into the waistband.
4. Staple a long ribbon to each side of the waistband (c).

140

Mexican Hat Dance

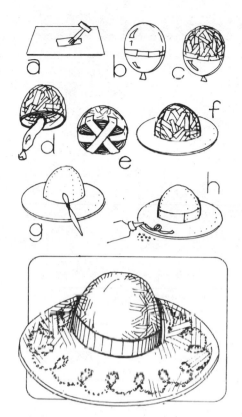

The word for "hat" in Spanish is *sombrero*. People in Mexico wear large sombreros to keep themselves cool in the hot sun. You can dance around a sombrero in the "Mexican Hat Dance."

Things You Need

newspaper • waxed paper • paste
large round balloon
poster board • scissors
poster paints • paintbrush
white liquid glue
glitter • ribbon

1. Place torn newspaper strips on waxed paper. Brush paste on one side (a).
2. Lay a row of pasted strips around the center of a blown-up balloon (b)
3. Cover the top half of the balloon with three layers of strips (c). This is the crown.
4. Remove the balloon when the paper is dry (d).
5. Glue three long newspaper strips across the opening of the crown (e).
6. Cut out a large circle from poster board.
7. Glue the crown centered on the circle to form the sombrero (f)
8. Paint the crown (g).
9. Decorate the sombrero with glitter added to glue. Glue ribbon around the crown (h).
10. Make up a dance to go with a little Mexican music. And dance around the sombrero on the floor.

Tarantella Tambourine

The tarantella is a lively Italian folk dance. Dancers and musicians often use the tambourine to keep the fast beat. The tambourine is a member of the drum family of percussion instruments. Most tambourines have jingle disks attached to them.

Things You Need

2 lightweight paper plates
small jingle bells
paper punch • narrow ribbons
crayons or markers

1. Punch several holes around the rim of a plate (a).
2. Mark where the holes fall on the rim of a second plate (b). Punch out.
3. With jingle bell inside, paste the plates together. The holes should line up.

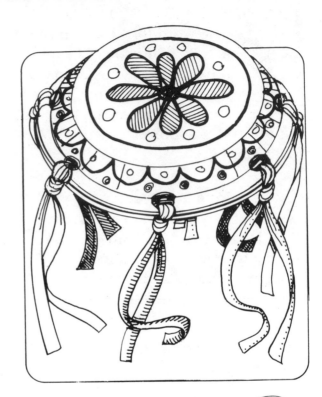

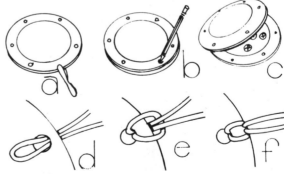

Dancing Fingers

When she was in Wonderland, Alice learned about the Lobster Quadrille. Sea creatures form a long line along the seashore, after the jellyfish are cleared away. Each takes a lobster for a dance partner. Create your own quadrille by letting your fingers dance.

Things You Need

paper • crayons or markers
scissors

1. Draw lobsters, turtles, crabs, and other sea creatures on paper with crayons or markers. Cut them out.
2. Cut two holes into the bottom of each creature to fit your fingers.
3. Put your fingers into the holes and move them in lively dance steps.

Tap Dance Sound Effects

Tap dancers have metal plates attached to the bottom of their shoes, at the toes and heels. But when you hear tap dancers in movies, these tapping sounds are usually created in the movie studios. Sound effect technicians tap with wooden spoons or metal cups. The next time you listen to music, tap dance along with your hands.

Things You Need
1 or 2 aluminum soft drink cans
hard surface

First try to tap out the sound effects of tap dancing with one can on a hard surface, like a cutting board. After you learn to do it well with one hand, try to create the sound of a tapping pair of shoes using two cans.

Experiment with other items, like wooden spoons or plastic bottle caps.

ON WITH THE SHOW

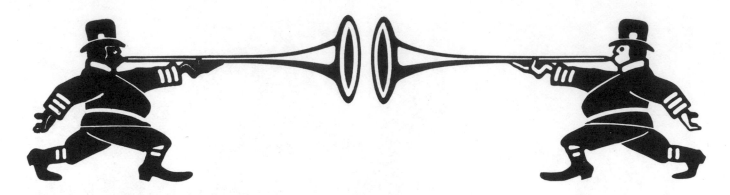

That's Entertainment

Welcome, girls and boys of all ages. I'm **Sharp**. I'm your master of ceremonies for this last chapter. Are you ready to be entertained? If you are, blow the horns, raise the curtains, and let the show begin.

Today people go to the theater to see dance performances. Ballet dancers dance on their toes.

Traveling shows once moved plays and music from theaters to small towns. Actors and singers carried their costumes, scenery, and musical instruments in wagons pulled by horses.

The circus has acrobats, calliope music, dancing elephants, and the boom, boom of the bass drum.

The marionette singers and dancers in puppet theaters are made of wood and attached to strings.

An orchestra can have over a hundred musicians. A group may have seven players.

And everyone loves the amusement park carousel with calliope music.

Organic Grinder Monkey

Animals entertain people. Many organ grinders have a monkey to help them. The monkey dances and does all kinds of tricks while the organ grinder cranks his hand organ to make music. After the show, the monkey collects pennies in his hat. Start your own monkey business with this hand organ and monkey.

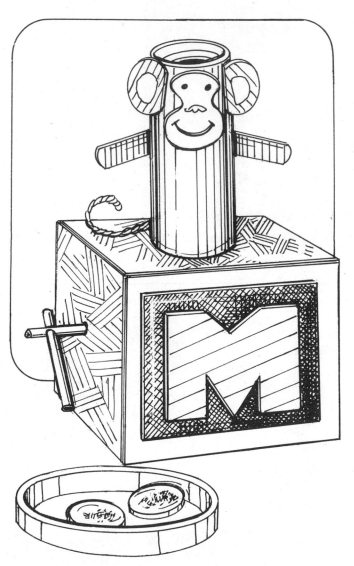

Things You Need

milk or juice carton
scissors • colored paper • paste
tape • pencil • drinking straw
paper punch • toilet tissue tube
pipe cleaner • jar lid

1. Cut away the bottom of a milk carton for the box (a and b).
2. Cut colored paper to fit on all sides of the box (c).
3. Paste the papers to the sides of the box. Add a paper design on the front of the box (d).
4. Twist a sharpened pencil into one side of the box to make a hole (e).
5. For the handle, cut a drinking straw into two pieces, one longer than the other. Punch a hole into the center of the short straw with a paper punch. Push the end of the long straw through the hole (f).
6. Push the handle into the hole on the side of the box.
7. Tape brown paper around a toilet tissue tube. Tape on arms (g).
8. Paste ears and a monkey face on the front of the tube.
9. Stand the monkey on the box. Use a jar lid for the monkey's pennies.
10. For a music box, decorate the tube like a clown.

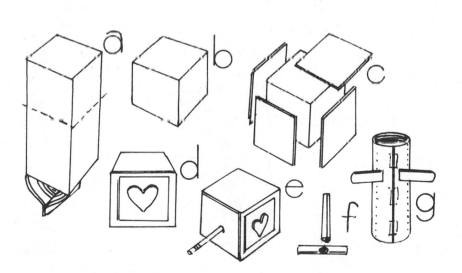

Snake Charmer

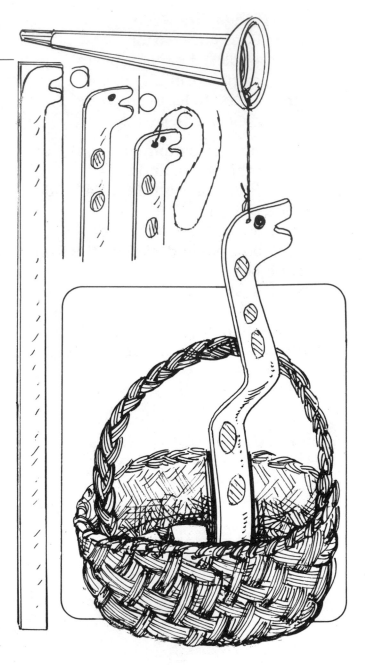

Every country has its own sidewalk entertainment. In India, the snake charmer is a crowd pleaser. A snake comes out of a basket when its master blows a horn. Actually, it's the moving horn, and not the music, that catches the snake's attention.

Things You Need
toy horn
long strip of felt or fabric
scissors • crayons or markers
string • tape • basket

1. Cut a snake's head into one end of a long strip of felt or fabric (a).
2. Draw eyes and spots on the strip with crayons or markers (b).
3. Make a small hole in the top of the head.
4. Tie one end of a long string into the hole (c). Tape the other end inside a horn.
5. Fold up the snake inside a basket. Lift the horn as you blow it to make the snake rise.

150

Munchkin Finger Puppets

The first movies had no sound. Many movie theaters had a piano player who played along with the action on the screen. Today, most movies have background music. In movie musicals, the actors sing. The *Wizard of Oz* is a popular musical movie. When Dorothy landed in Oz, she met the Munchkins, who welcomed her with a happy song.

Things You Need
colored paper • scissors
crayons or markers • tape
your hand

1. Cut five pieces of flesh-colored or plain paper. Make them as tall as your middle finger and long enough to wrap around it, plus a little extra.
2. In the middle of four of these pieces of paper, draw different Munchkin faces and clothes (a).
3. Roll each paper into a tube and tape it closed (b). The tubes should be able to fit over your fingers.
4. Draw Dorothy on the remaining paper. Roll and tape her into a tube.
5. Place Dorothy on your thumb and the Munchkins on your fingers. Move your fingers and make them talk and sing in high Munchkin voices.

Clown Radio

With the invention of the radio, entertainment moved into homes. Families no longer had to go to theaters to see plays or movies. They could hear music and plays in their own living rooms. This silly radio is lots of fun.

Things You Need
deep box (saltine or graham cracker box)
colored paper • scissors • paste
pencil • lightweight fabric
crayons or markers
small pocket radio

1. Cut away the flaps from the opened end of a deep box. This end will be at the bottom.

2. Cut colored paper large enough to wrap around the box (a). If the box is too big, cut paper to fit on each side. Also cut paper to fit on the top.
3. Paste or tape the cut paper to the box.
4. Lightly draw a large circle on the front of the box near the bottom.
5. Cut out the circle (b).
6. Cut from lightweight fabric a circle larger than the hole on the box (c).
7. Paste the fabric circle over the hole on the inside of the box (d).
8. Paste on paper hair. Also add a drawn or paper face and radio dials (e).
9. Turn on the radio and place the clown over it. The radio's speaker should face the clown's mouth.

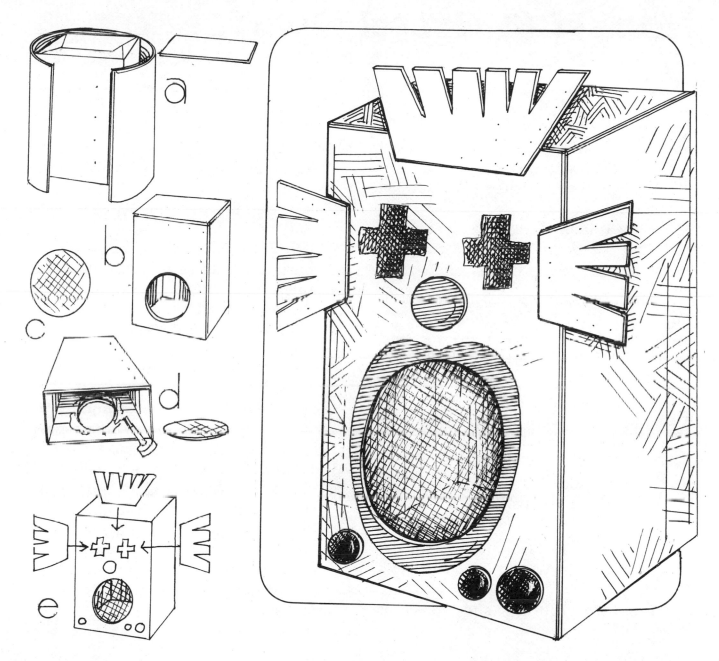

a

b

c

d

e

153

Hansel & Gretel Opera

 Opera is the marriage of all the arts because it has music, singing, acting, and dance. Composer Engelbert Humperdinck wrote an opera about the favorite folktale of Hansel and Gretel.

Would you like to create your own opera? That's easy. All you need are puppets, a story, and good vocal cords.

To complete your opera, consult the projects that follow: Woodsman, Stepmother & Witch; Opera Stage; and Scenery, Libretto & Production.

Things You Need
2 small empty plastic dishwashing detergent bottles
cardboard • yarn • scissors
white liquid glue • fabric
ribbon • crayons

1. Remove the label from two plastic detergent bottles. Wash the bottles thoroughly.
2. Wrap yarn around a short piece of cardboard for Hansel's hair. Use a longer piece of cardboard for Gretel's hair.
3. Tie the yarn together at one end (a). Cut through the yarn at the other end (see arrow in a).
4. Glue hair to the bottom of each bottle (b). Dry.
5. Cut fabric for each puppet's skirt or shirt. It should be as tall as the bottle and long enough to wrap around it, plus a little extra.
6. Wrap the fabric skirt or shirt loosely around the bottles.
7. Tie the skirt or shirt in place with ribbon (c).
8. Draw a face on Hansel and Gretel with crayons (d). You can also paste on paper faces.
9. To work the puppets, slip your hand under the skirt or shirt. Either put your index finger into the neck of the bottle or hold the neck in your hand. Move the puppet when you speak. You can play with both puppets yourself or have a friend work the other puppet.

Woodsman, Stepmother & Witch

Besides Hansel and Gretel, other characters are in the opera. Their father is a poor woodsman. When the family is starving, the stepmother suggests that they abandon the children in the woods. The wicked witch lives deep in the woods in a house made of candy.

Things You Need

supplies for Hansel and Gretel
(p. 154)

Woodsman (A)

Glue black hair and beard to his face. Make his shirt brown.

Stepmother (B)

Glue pieces of gray yarn for her hair. Make her skirt from printed fabric.

Witch (C)

Make her skirt black. Create hat from black felt rolled into a cone and trimmed.

Opera Stage

You can't have an opera without a stage. This one is perfect for hiding the puppeteers.

Things You Need
supplies for Limbo Pole
large piece of fabric
safety pins, needle and thread,
or stapler

1. Follow directions for making the Limbo Pole (p. 139). Tape a loop to each pole near the top.
2. Set up the poles with the broom handle resting in the loops, taped close to the top of the poles.
3. Cut a large piece of fabric for the curtain. (You could use an old sheet.) Make it as wide as the distance from pole to pole and as long as from the broom handle to the floor, plus a little extra.
4. Fold the top edge of the fabric over the pole. Secure it with safety pins or by sewing it.

Scenery, Libretto & Production

Scenery

The scenery in an opera helps to tell the story. You can't enjoy the story of Hansel and Gretel without the house made out of candy!

Things You Need

cardboard • colored paper
crayons or markers • scissors
paste • sticks • strong tape

1. Using colored paper and crayons, draw: (A) Hansel and Gretel's house, (B) two trees, (C) witch's candy house, (D) cage, (E) oven.

2. Paste cutout scenery on cardboard. Cut out.
3. Tape a stick, like a twig or a dowel, to the back of each.
4. Insert the sticks into the top of the stage's side poles when they are needed.

Libretto and Production

1. The story of an opera is called the *libretto*. Look for a book about Hansel and Gretel, at your library.
2. Divide the story into three acts: (A) the children's house, (B) the forest, and (C) the witch's house.

A   B   C   D   E

3. Write down the words that each singer will sing. Use the exact words in the story plus add your own. Identify each singer with his or her stage name, for instance:

Hansel——This door tastes delicious.
Gretel——The windowsill is yummy.
Witch——Who is eating my house?!

4. Make a photocopy of the libretto for each singer.
5. Each part can be sung any way the singer wants to sing it. Some lines can be sung to familiar melodies like "All around the Mulberry Bush" and "Old MacDonald." Sing in different voices.

Swan Song

Hi, it's me again, **G Clef**. I hope you have enjoyed your musical adventure. We have discovered so many things to see and do and so many ways to make sounds and songs. And you will have more fun each time you open *Music Crafts for Kids*.

It is now time for the eight notes, their friends, and me to sing our "swan song" and take our final bow. It is time for *you* to continue your musical discovery in school, at home, at camp, and anywhere music fills the air. Remember, we will always be with you whenever you listen to your favorite music or sing your favorite songs.

Index